THE ASTONISHMENT OF WORDS

the
Astonishment
of Words

AN EXPERIMENT IN THE COMPARISON OF LANGUAGES

BY VICTOR PROETZ

Foreword by Alastair Reid

Afterword by Charles Nagel

UNIVERSITY OF TEXAS PRESS, AUSTIN AND LONDON

ACKNOWLEDGMENTS

"J'ai perdu, l'autre jour, un monde." Reprinted by permission of the publishers from Fernand Baldensperger, *D'Edmond Spenser à Alan Seeger.* Cambridge, Mass.: Harvard University Press, copyright 1938, 1966, by the President and Fellows of Harvard College.

"Le Jaseroque," by Frank Lord Warrin, Jr. Reprinted by permission; copyright © 1931, 1959 The New Yorker Magazine, Inc.

"Look, stranger, on this island now." Copyright 1937 and renewed 1965 by W. H. Auden. Reprinted from *Collected Shorter Poems 1927–1957,* by W. H. Auden, by permission of Random House, Inc. and Faber and Faber Ltd.

"Sonette aus dem Portugiesischen," 1, 6, 22. From *Uebertragungen, Gesammelte Werke* by Rainer Maria Rilke, copyright 1930 by Suhrkamp Verlag. Reprinted by permission of Suhrkamp Verlag.

"Stephen's Green." Reprinted with permission of The Macmillan Company from *Collected Poems* by James Stephens. Copyright 1915 by The Macmillan Company, renewed 1943 by James Stephens. Translations by James Joyce reprinted by permission of The Society of Authors as representatives of the Estate of James Joyce.

"the hours rise up putting off stars." Copyright 1923, 1951 by E. E. Cummings. Reprinted and translated from *Poems 1923–1954* by E. E. Cummings by permission of Harcourt Brace Jovanovich, Inc. and from *Complete Poems 1913–1935* by E. E. Cummings by permission of MacGibbon and Kee Ltd.

"Sweeney among the Nightingales." From *Collected Poems 1909–1962* by T. S. Eliot. Copyright 1936 by Harcourt Brace Jovanovich, Inc.; copyright © 1963, 1964 by T. S. Eliot. Reprinted by permission of Harcourt Brace Jovanovich, Inc. and Faber and Faber Ltd.

International Standard Book Number 0–292–70116–0
Library of Congress Catalog Card Number 71–144140
Copyright © 1971 by James R. Billman
All Rights Reserved

Typesetting and printing by The University of Texas Printing Division, Austin

Bound by Universal Bookbindery, Inc., San Antonio

TO THE MEMORY OF
Nathaniel Burton Paradise
AND TO
Margaret Bowditch Woodford Paradise
AND
Peter and Deborah
WITH LOVE

CONTENTS

FOREWORD

Books are generally the result of a certain design, a certain deliberation. This book, however, is less the fulfilment of an intention than a fortuitous accident, less a book than a wavelength, and I feel less disposed to introducing it formally than to celebrating its existence, wistfully, for it obliges me to write about Victor Proetz in the past tense when, of all the dead people I know, he is the most vividly alive—I am able to hear his voice at whim, and to read him or think of him generates a continuing conversation. But even those who are reading him for the first time will make something of the same discovery—his writing is idiosyncratically personal, funny, outrageous, and his subject less of a crystallization than a discovery which properly belongs to whoever wants to take it over and translate it into his own curiosity.

I first met Victor Proetz in Scotland in 1948, and knew him from that point until he died in 1966, yet I find it hard to isolate single occasions from that time, for in fact we embarked on an endless conversation which paid little regard to place and time, perhaps because whatever the substance of our conversation, we were always talking about words, trying them out, exploring their possibilities. But it was not that he was interested in words to the exclusion of what they were used to say—it was precisely the oddness of words as a vehicle that absorbed him endlessly, and he could not see how anybody should use them without astonishment, could take them for granted. Words astounded him by their very existence. He looked on them as a separate race, small Martians with their own nature, and with a changing existence much more durable than that of us who used

them. He did not throw words about so much as use them as though
they would stay in the air. He turned words over in his head, he
listened to them, he unraveled them, he looked them up, he played
with them, he passed them on like presents, all with an unjadeable
astonishment. I think most of his friendships were founded on this
wavelength, on a disposition to talk for the pleasure of talking, to
explore language-astonishments, to play games seriously. The practice of architecture, his professional life, he kept meticulously private; but his friendships were spun out around that curious, outrageous, probing, affecting wit of his, which became a kind of web these
friends grew to inhabit, so that they could meet one another on VP's
wavelength. I have often seen him begin to talk to someone he had
just met, with great attention and meticulous politeness until he found
a thread of humor; from that point on, he quite simply enwound who-
ever-it-was with words. He realized all this, of course, and in time
he came to refer to this web of his own winding as the Games. We all
played the Games. It was what his friendship demanded, and it was he
who either set the games in motion, or codified them, or ran them
even when absent, like a ghostly and outrageous Marquis of Queens-
bury. I think VP found the game-context to be the easiest one to
inhabit. His own taste was absolute, arrogantly so; but to connect
with people on the level of humor and wit and words bypassed any
complexities of confrontation. But his web wound in a great variety
of people, and it remains in the atmosphere. His round way of saying,
his ripe voice, his *style* hung on in the air and lore of every house he
visited; the Games themselves we keep on playing and being.

One of these Games is this book. (The other Games might easily
have been books, but they remained unwritten because they already
existed, and were always being changed, adapted, added to, and
played.) This particular Game began just as VP describes it, a question mark that crossed his mind and stayed there. Just what do other
languages make of the quirky idioms of English, and of those texts
which embed themselves in our language-memory below the level of
meaning? Are nursery rhymes translatable? (I was recently track-
ing down the idiom 'once in a blue moon' in Spanish, and found it
rendered in one dictionary as *a cada muerte de obispo*—every time

a bishop dies.) VP seized on the behemoth with a cry of joy, and his
conversations from then on were punctuated with the discoveries
that follow in this text. And yet he did not set out to write a book,
but saw his notes as a by-product of a continuing curiosity, and saw
quite correctly that no book would ever take care of the subject, but
would rather set it in motion. Games belong to no one but the players.
The present book, in fact, is probably not at all what VP would have
published had he been alive to do the editing himself, and had he
ever envisioned an end or even a stopping place in his investigations.
He despised deadlines and specifications—there was, or there ought
to be, all the time in the world. What he did do was to outline a list
of poems and texts with the intention of exploring their fates in translation. Some of these would have led nowhere, but others would
have yielded him more of those oblique, whimsical, and brilliant
notes which he added by way of commentary. It might have taken
him even further, for he talked of reversing the process and following French and German texts through their consequences in English;
and I had sent him some Spanish versions of T. S. Eliot which led
him to consider adding Spanish to his investigations. He combed
the language-memories of those he met, and his projected list of contents grew much faster than his finished commentaries. For him, the
work was ancient, useless, and timeless—in short, a Game; and he
might have resisted finishing it, for that would have meant putting a
frame round what was an endless, random activity. To some, books
and deadlines are useful allies, to others, enemies to be outwitted.
The present volume is a fragment, a residue, an accretion, a work
of salvage, containing only those comparative translations which VP
had tracked down and provided with a written commentary—but it
is obvious that the book itself could have become an endless series.
There is nothing particularly new in discovering the vagaries of comparative translation, but what VP adds is the dimension of awe, the
astonishment that translation is possible at all. VP disavowed ex-
plicitly and respectfully any claim to being a scholar, and yet his is
precisely the kind of enthusiastic curiosity which gives scholarship
its pointers. But his commentaries are marvelous pieces of writing in
themselves, cranky, laconic, outrageous, subtle, and very funny, so

close to his way of talking, so infectious in their tone, that the reader quickly becomes an addict and finds himself wondering over the fate of texts as diverse as Tennyson in Serbo-Croat or *My Fair Lady* in Russian. The book instinctively translates itself back into active curiosity.

Anyone who moves between languages discovers a whole nether world inhabited by translators, interpreters, crossers of frontiers, a world whose realities are often in doubt, a kind of limbo which quivers in the relativity of languages. Through knowing more than one language, we become aware that the words we fasten to the visible world are totally arbitrary; and a vast gulf opens between words and what is beyond them. This has the effect of setting free the words themselves, of making us more conscious of their odd nature, more disposed to play and take risks with them. I think that it also increases our awe over both the act of saying and the unsayable. I would quite often send to VP instances of both dazzling translation and appalling mistranslation, which he would match in reply. Even now when I come across other instances, he comes immediately to mind. I remember calling on him more than once and finding him at his writing table, spectacles on the end of his nose, fingers in three dictionaries at once, rumbling out in lieu of a greeting, "Wouldn't you have thought that somebody would have thought of a thoroughly English way to say *vice versa* instead of just *vice versa*? I've prepared three candidate-phrases. Listen . . ."

VP was the center of a charmed and word-struck circle into which this book invites its readers. I doubt that anyone who reads it will be able to resist going on writing it, nudged by its attendant spirit. Even now, as I write, I am acutely aware, not only of VP's voice and wavelength, but emphatically of the fact that none of us who were his friends would use words with the same keen pleasure, the same meticulous care, the same astonishment, had we not known him.

ALASTAIR REID

The Game

ALL THIS BEGAN in New Haven after supper one Sunday night in the middle Thirties, when Burton Paradise came up with "Voici l'hippopotame," which I still think is the funniest thing I have ever heard. He was reading aloud to us and we all sat there rocking with laughter. He was reading the Bible in French. I didn't know until years later that the wonderful nonsense we were playing with was the result of their having read out Clarence Day the Sunday night before, when I wasn't there.

To me "Behold now behemoth" has all the breath-taking splendor of the Sistine Chapel. "Behemoth"—listen to it! The very word is drawn at the same overwhelming scale as Michelangelo's ceiling, and is practically in the same style. But in French they haven't even got him in the least Old-Testament-looking. He is no more splendid than an ordinary one is. I cannot seem to get the meaning of this phrase blown up to anything more monumental than "Here is the hippopotamus," which is no more monumental than "I see the cat."

I remember some scholars saying that night that this kind of thing was entirely the fault of the Académie Française. The Académie has kept the language of the French so pure for everybody that nowadays there is almost no way of squeezing a really decent archaic effect out of it. I gathered that there was no archaic French any longer because it was forbidden—anyway, something like that.

But Hebrew was not forbidden by the Académie, was it? And besides, wouldn't the French translation of the Bible have been made before the 1630's, or whenever it was that Cardinal Richelieu and his literary friends took over? Then it was not the Académie that kept the French from sticking to Hebrew as the rest of us did. The Vul-

gate says "Ecce behemoth," and even the Germans stick to it in spite
of all their prejudices. "Siehe da den Behemoth" is the way you say
it in German. *Hippopotame* indeed! They must have liked it that way.

Then they have "Heureux les débonnaires." Fancy that! That is the
way the French say "Blessed are the meek."

The first time I remember hearing the word *débonnaire* at all, it
was Milton who said it.

> Fill'd her with thee a daughter fair,
> So bucksom, blith, and debonair.

I have always loved that very much, but I have certainly always
thought of that child of Aurora's as being a bouncing, blue-eyed baby
girl, very amiable and very sweet. Even in his day Noah Webster
defined it as "affable, courteous, graceful and gay." How did he—and
I—get that idea, when to a French person Aurora's little baby would
have been only buxom, blithe, and *meek*? And now, incidentally,
that *débonnaire* means "meek," how do you say "debonair" in French?
Here's how:

> *il la fit mère de toi, fille charmante,*
> *si enjouée, rieuse et gracieuse.*

Here is an example of another thing that happens to French. "Au
Clair de la Lune" was originally

> *Au clair de la lune,*
> *Mon ami Pierrot,*
> *Prête-moi ta lume . . .*

But when the word *lume* faded out of the language and "was no
longer understood," "lend me your light" became "lend me your
pen," and "mon ami Pierrot" was no longer the moon itself. He became a third person—the person with the pen—and the little poem,
inadvertently, became a little parody of itself. Why did they allow
that to happen? Even I can understand *lume* perfectly well.

The French have the curious national characteristic of being stone
deaf to borderline pronunciations. Once, in the Gare D'Orléans, I
stood in a queue behind an American lady who wanted a ticket to

Orléans, which she pronounced as we do when we say New Orleans. Between them two ticket sellers could not conjure up the foggiest notion of what she was trying to say, until I helped them out. Any of us can understand a Frenchman, even though he wants a ticket to Tschick-ah-*geau*. I don't know why.

Anyway, you have had your first taste of what we are getting ourselves into.

German translators come through with some pretty crashing effects too, but in their own, inimitable way. How can a self-respecting German person with any ear at all for Scotland be led into thinking that "Grün werden nun die Binsen, oh!" could possibly be acceptable to anyone as a translation of "Green Grow the Rashes, O"? (It isn't in this book, for instance.) I have discovered in a footnote that somewhere there is a Swiss-German translation of it. When I find it—if I can read it at all—I certainly expect to find some racy trace of *das etwas Schottländisches* left in it. A Frenchwoman I know once told me that she had heard French spoken with an Alabama accent. "It gets to be a kind of Basque," she said. Maybe it will be something like that.

How do you say "Yankee Doodle" in French—in case you can? Does "The snail's on the thorn" get to be about an *escargot*? If you want to say "Fourscore and seven years ago" in French, how can you keep from saying "*Quatre-vingt-sept années* ago," in the ordinary way? How do they say "Houyhnhnm" and "Cheshire Cat" and things like that in German? How well does Hamlet come through with that soliloquy of his in any language but his own? (I had no idea that simply everybody had taken a crack at translating that.) How can you keep a phrase like "La Belle Dame sans merci" in a French translation of the poem from being lost in the surrounding French? And how, in God's name, can you possibly say "There she blows!" I couldn't wait to find out. So I sat up in bed one of those nights and made a list of everything I wanted to hear the sound of in French and in German—a very much too long one. Next morning I added all the things I had forgotten to put down. Imagine forgetting *all* of them! This list, ruthlessly cut over a stretch of time, I began to think, could become the table of contents for a book—in case I had the energy to undertake such a book. How, I should have thought instead, do you say "Smiling the boy fell dead"?

After lunch the next day, because it was nearby, I went to the New Haven Public Library for a preliminary look around. A few days later I went in to the New York Public Library to talk to some librarians and to putter around there. Then I called all the German and French bookstores in the New York Classified Telephone Directory and told them that I was in search of an anthology of English "gems" translated into German and French. And what was the name of this anthology, they asked me. They had never heard of such a thing. Neither had I. There wasn't any. So I began to buy books from them and to order up others from publishers abroad. Soon I had eight or ten new feet of books piling up on the floor. Some of them contained smatterings of the things I wanted. Then I went to the libraries at Yale and to the Library of Congress, and spent a few more weeks poking around in them. So there I was, two months later, up to the ears in notes.

If only a proper scholar had undertaken this book in the first place, I kept thinking, I could have bought it the very first day and found out everything I wanted to know. By this time it would be in its logical place in a bookcase next to Palgrave and *The Oxford Book of English Verse*. But no proper scholar had. He had never thought of such a thing, and I cannot imagine why not. What I manage to put together here, I went on thinking in despair, will be fit only for guest rooms—and isn't that depressing?

I began to try to work the thing out. All this is fascinating, of course, but it's going to be a whale of a job. It will take me at least a month—maybe two—just to make a notebook of the stuff I can find. Wasn't that *débonnaire*?

I was in the midst of copying out *The Mikado* in a dingy room where one is not permitted to smoke, when I suddenly knew I was going to carry this thing through in spite of hell, no matter how long it took. And it was about then that I knew that any cross section of mine was going to be a pretty zigzag thing. But isn't it lucky, I went on thinking, that this Game doesn't require any scholarship at all, because if it did I couldn't be playing it.

That's true. You won't need very much German or French—and you don't need both, certainly—to have fun out of the cream of this. I have only some children's German left from years ago—all very foggy and threadbare—and only about as much of the kind of pathetic kitchen- or pig-French as a man needs to get through a few schools and things, and to ask French chambermaids to bring him up a morsel of ice, if there is any.

I have not chosen the examples you would have chosen. How do I know which ones yours are? But at the end of each article I am giving you some unobtrusive footnotes—which is more than anybody has done for me—and I am giving you a bibliography so that, without too much trouble, you can look up the rest of anything here that interests you particularly. And I am giving you the Game itself to go on playing forever in your own way.

Such a book would be intended for all of *us*—not for scholars at all—by one of us who always likes or dislikes almost everything a little bit too much; who has badly-thought-out prejudices about all the wrong things, which he hopes never quite to outgrow; who loves to be enchanted by experts—from a distance—preferably from a seat in the fourth row on the aisle. If you find him forgetting himself and being disrespectful to his betters now and then, never mind. Let it go. The only essential difference between him and those tiresome people who don't know anything about music but know what they like, is that he doesn't even know what he likes.

I *think* he has nothing to prove—which is ambitious enough for anybody.

VICTOR PROETZ

The Illustrations

ANONYMOUS

Rune of Hospitality

(*From the Gaelic*)

I saw a stranger yestereen;
I put food in the eating place,
Drink in the drinking place,
Music in the listening place:
And, in the sacred name of the Triune,
He blessed myself and my house,
My cattle and my dear ones.
And the lark said in her song,
    Often, often, often,
Goes the Christ in the stranger's guise:
    Often, often, often,
Goes the Christ in the stranger's guise.

Recorded by Kenneth Macleod

Altgälische Rune von der Gastfreundschaft

Ich sah einen Fremden gestern.
Ich trug ihm ein Mahl in den Speise-Saal,
Trunk in den Trink-Saal,
Musik in den Lauscher-Saal.
Und im heiligen Namen der Dreieinigkeit
Segnete er mich und mein Haus,
Mein Vieh und meine Lieben.
Und die Lerche sagte in ihrem Gesang:
    Oft, oft, oft

Geht Christus im Kleide des Fremden;
   Oft, oft, oft
Geht Christus im Kleide des Fremden.

Translated by Käthe Braun-Prager

Rune de l'hospitalité

J'ai vu un étranger le soir passé;
Je lui ai porté à manger dans la place du manger,
Et à boire dans la place du boire,
La musique dans la place d'écouter:
Et au nom sacré de la Trinité
Il me bénit, moi et ma maison,
Mes bêtes et ceux que j'aime.
Et l'alouette dans son chant disait:
   Souvent, souvent, souvent,
Marche le Christ en guise d'étranger:
   Souvent, souvent, souvent,
Marche le Christ en guise d'étranger.

Translated by Margaret Paradise and Deborah Paradise Custer

IT WOULD HAVE BEEN PLEASANT to start off these experiments with "Sumer is icumen in," as everybody else does, but I have found no translation of it into any other language at all.

The "Cuckoo Song" is a rota for four voices accompanied by two deeper voices. It is one of the earliest English lyrics known and is probably the most remarkable secular composition left to us from the first half of the thirteenth century. The famous words are so intricately involved with the music that there would be no point in disentangling them from the four-part canon for display in another language. Unsung, they are scarcely more than a list of archaically delightful, evocative, singable summer things. Besides, from its earliest beginnings, every language has had incantations of its own for bringing back summer.

I do not know whether the "Rune of Hospitality" is well known or not. It was published first "sometime before 1927" in *The Celtic Review*. I saw it first in 1948 in Scotland at St. Andrews. It was printed on a single leaf of paper. When I asked my host, who was a student at the university, what it was, he didn't know. He could not remember where it came from nor how he happened to have it. Seven years later in New York I came onto it again, this time in German, in an anthology of English verse in translation.

Kenneth Macleod had listened all his life to the old songs and to the recitations of ancient poetry in the remote, unvisited islands of the Hebrides. In the introduction to *The Road to the Isles*, it is said that he made his "Rune of Hospitality" by joining two Gaelic fragments together. These—and this is not altogether clear to me—he had heard sung. Does this mean that he had heard half of two tunes, the other halves of both of which had been lost? This is a curious thing if that is the way it was. Did different people sing the fragments in different places? He must, in any event, have had to disregard the two fragments of tune when he set the fragments of verse together.

I was afraid at first that this poem could not properly be thought of as a candidate for this book, since the fragments were Gaelic to begin with and not English. Then I changed to thinking we were really concerned here with Macleod's poem in English. If Macleod becomes "Anonymous" simply because he deals with folk tunes, what is to become of Burns? But I wanted so very much to have the "Rune" among "Edward" and the "Corbies," where I think it belongs, that in the end I put it there—and by "in the end" I mean ten minutes later.

(That's the trouble with this book and with this man, you will say —they are both unreasonable now and then.)

There can be no doubt that Frau Braun-Prager's "Altgälische Rune von der Gastfreundschaft" is a translation from Macleod. She can scarcely have wandered the Hebrides on her own to discover and put together the same two fragments in exactly the way he did, although in *Die Lyra des Orpheus,* in which her poem appears, there is no mention of Kenneth Macleod.

In the Braun-Prager translation, "song" becomes "Gesang," which is finer than "Lied" would have been, but "Kleide" is not so fine as "guise." It lacks the meaning and the miracle of "guise." "Oft," of course, is a necessity, not a departure, but it sounds to me very lark-like, even with a single syllable.

Mrs. Paradise and her daughter, who undertook the translation into French for me, since I could find none ready made, have been discerning enough to see eye to eye with Frau Braun-Prager in trans-lating "song" as "chant" rather than as "chanson," and to stand by the Reverend Mr. Macleod with "guise."

This poem is wonderfully successful and beautiful in all three lan-guages. I point this out because in this book, unhappily, so satisfying a triple balance is rare.

To fill the gaps where a few translations I particularly wanted did not exist, I have been obliged to fall back on my friends—on myself, even. By gaps I mean a number of instances where a German *or* a French translation was to be had, but not both. I was in hopes, of course, of finding all my samples already translated, because what I wanted particularly to know was how these great traditions of ours had been presented over the years, to all the French- and German-speaking people who had no English and were obliged to get their impressions of English literature from something that wasn't quite it. Now I know. What they have been given instead, in many cases, is hardly to be compared with the adequate Roman copies of Greek sculpture that we have all been brought up with.

Some of the translations in this book have been made by the great-est possible masters—almost invariably by masters of the language into which, rather than out of which, their translations have been made. Some are by inspired lesser masters; some by accomplished, graceful amateurs. (One of these, a gentle German Wall Street broker of the nineteenth century, translated some English and Ameri-can poetry of his period into German and had it privately printed for his children and his grandchildren. He has not done it brilliantly at all, but he has done it very nicely.) The worst are by publishers' relatives and various hacks who have no taste and only the most elementary sense of English. This kind of bluffing is pernicious mischief.

Translation at best is rarely what is called "rewarding." Things made of words get out of joint in the moving and, no matter how skillful he may be ordinarily, nor "on which rung of the ladder he stands," the translator is half doomed before he begins.

It is impossible to lay the pattern of one language onto that of another and make it fit. The second language is dead against it. Instead, devious means must be contrived for getting through the barriers into the style of the second language in some other way. Not only must the translator come through with the proper words, he must re-create all the music, all the architecture, all the color schemes, and all the light and shade and shadow of the first language in the style of the second. Anyone who dares to pour the precious stuff "from the golden shell into the silver" is taking a great risk.

In spite of what I am saying here, the complete success of some of these translations is incredible. They have weathered all the agony of change, and have come through it in full bloom. A few, a very few—and I hope I can be restrained enough not to point them out when we get to them—have actually improved on their way through hell.

ANONYMOUS

The Three Ravens

(*English Version*)

I.

There were three rauens sat on a tree,
  Downe a downe, hay down, hay downe
There were three rauens sat on a tree,
  With a downe
There were three rauens sat on a tree,
They were as blacke as they might be.
  With a downe derrie, derrie, derrie, downe, downe

II.

The one of them said to his mate,
"Where shall we our breakfast take?"

III.

"Down in yonder greene field,
There lies a knight slain vnder his shield.

IV.

"His hounds they lie downe at his feete,
So well they can their master keepe.

V.

"His haukes they flie so eagerly,
There's no fowle dare him come nie."

VI.

Downe there comes a fallow doe,
As great with yong as she might goe.

VII.

She lift vp his bloudy hed,
And kist his wounds that were so red.

VIII.

She got him vp vpon her backe,
And carried him to earthen lake.

IX.

She buried him before the prime,
She was dead herselfe ere euen-song time.

X.

God send euery gentleman,
[Downe a downe, hay down, hay downe]
God send euery gentleman,
[With a downe]
God send euery gentleman
Such haukes, such hounds, and such a leman.
[With a downe derrie, derrie, derrie, downe, downe]

The Twa Corbies

(*Scottish Version*)

I.

As I was walking all alane
I heard twa corbies making a mane:
The tane unto the tither did say,
"Whar sall we gang and dine the day?"

II.

"In behint yon auld fail dyke
I wot there lies a new-slain knight;
And naebody kens that he lies there
But his hawk, and his hound, and his lady fair.

III.

"His hound is to the hunting gane,
His hawk to fetch the wild-fowl hame,

His lady's ta'en anither mate,
So we may mak' our dinner sweet.

IV.

"Ye'll sit on his white hause-bane,
And I'll pike out his bonny blue e'en:
Wi' ae lock o' his gowden hair
We'll theek our nest when it grows bare.

V.

"Mony a one for him maks mane,
But nane sall ken whar he is gane:
O'er his white banes, when they are bare,
The wind sall blaw for evermair."

Die zwei Raben

(*Altschottische Ballade*)

[I.]

Als ich gar einsam bin gegangen,
Hört' ich zwei Raben, die Krächzen sangen,
Und einer zu dem andern sprach:
"Wo halten wir heute unser Gelag?"

[II.]

"Dort hinter dem grünen, grünen Hagen
Weiß ich einen Ritter frisch erschlagen,
Und keinem ist die Stelle kund,
Als seinem Liebchen und Falken und Hund.

[III.]

Sein Hund in Wald ist jagen gegangen,
Sein Falk, sich Federwild zu fangen,
Sein Lieb hat sich einem andern gesellt,
Und so ist uns Mahl bestellt.

[IV.]
Du auf den weißen Hals und Nachen,
Ich will die blauen Augen hacken,
Sein goldnes Haar, das nie verwest,
Soll wärmen unser kaltes Nest.

[V.]
Um ihn wird mancher sich betrüben,
Doch keiner wissen, wo er geblieben.
Über seine Gebeine weiß und bar
Soll wehen der Wind auf immerdar."

Translated by Karl Elze

Les Deux Corbeaux

Comme je me promenais tout seul, j'entendis deux corbeaux
se parler: l'un dit à son camarade: "Où irons-nous dîner aujourd'
hui?"

"Derrière ce vieux mur en terre, gît un chevalier nouvellement
tué, et personne ne sait qu'il gît en ce lieu, excepté son épervier,
son chien et sa dame.

"Son chien est allé à la chasse, son épervier lie pour un autre
maître les oiseaux sauvages; sa dame a pris un autre serviteur;
ainsi, nous pourrons faire un bon dîner.

"Toi, tu te percheras sur sa blanche poitrine; moi, je lui arra-
cherai avec mon bec ses beaux yeux bleus, et des boucles de ses
cheveux blonds nous boucherons les feutes de nos nids.

"De ses amis plus d'un mène grand deuil, mais nul ne saura
jamais où il est tombé; et sur ses os dépouilles et blanchis, les
vents souffleront toujours."

Translator unidentified

SIR WALTER SCOTT was familiar with "The Three Ravens" long before "The Twa Corbies," usually called the Scottish version, was
given him by Charles Kirkpatrick Sharpe, Esq., jun., of Hoddam
(near Edinburgh), who had copied it out for Sir Walter from another
copy "as written down by a lady," who had probably heard rather
than seen the ballad, since nobody attempting to explore the an-
tiquity of this version has ever got beyond this lady.

The Scottish version appeared in print for the first time in Scott's
Minstrelsy of the Scottish Border in the edition of 1802 or 1803.

Of the two, "The Three Ravens" has had a much longer recorded
history. Scott, who published the two versions side by side—as I am
doing it here—had "The Three Ravens" from Ritson's *Ancient Songs*
(1792), where both the tune and the words were re-published from
Ravencroft's *Melismata: Musicall Phansies, fitting the Court, Citie,
and Countrey Humours, to 3, 4, and 5 Voyces*, which was brought out
in London first in 1611. Scott agrees with Ritson that the ballad is
probably much older than that.

The third raven is left out of the Scottish version: he is super-
numerary at best since he has actually no part to play in the ballad.
The first four Scottish lines are essentially the same as they are in
English but from there on the plots begin to branch. The Scottish
ballad tells of a faithless lady and of traitorous animals, and ends in a
quatrain of the most utter desolation. The English one is embellished
at intervals with the voices singing lovely Elizabethan downe-hay-
down-hay-downes. Here the slain knight's lady bearing his unborn
child seems to have been cruelly bewitched and turned into a fallow
doe. Nobody has ever known quite how to account for this. It is in
this version that the knight's noble lady, his hawks and his hounds,
are faithful to him even after death. The doe carries her dead lover
on her back to "earthen lake," where she buries him before the prime
and "was dead herselfe ere euen-song time."

> God send euery gentleman
> Such haukes, such hounds, and such a leman.

The second raven's speech must end properly with the end of the fifth couplet. Some editions have the second raven speaking the ballad to the end. This is a mistake, at least for the last two lines. These are a benediction and benedictions are never to be associated with legendary ravens.

I have little fault to find with Herr Elze's splendid translation into German, although I question his choice of the word "Liebchen" as quite a suitable parallel to "lady" in line 8. A medieval lady can be unfaithful to a knight without forfeiting her dignity to the point of becoming his "sweetheart"—which is probably a second-class word in any language.

The French translator, to record "Les Deux Corbeaux" at all, was obliged to substitute five tight paragraphs of prose for the five Scottish quatrains. His effect is splendidly vivid and sinister but, unluckily, the ballad can never be sung.

ANONYMOUS

Edward, Edward

[I.]
Quhy dois zour brand sae drop wi' bluid,
     Edward, Edward?
Quhy dois zour brand sae drop wi' bluid?
   And quhy sae sad gang zee, O?
O, I hae killed my hauke sae guid,
     Mither, mither:
O, I hae killed my hauke sae guid;
   And I had nae mair bot hee, O.

[II.]
Zour haukis bluid was nevir sae reid,
     Edward, Edward,
Zour haukis bluid was nevir sae reid,
   My deir son I tell thee, O.
O, I hae killed my reid-roan steid,
     Mither, mither:
O, I hae killed my reid-roan steid,
   That erst was sae fair and free, O.

[III.]
Zour steid was auld, and ze hae gat mair,
     Edward, Edward
Zour steid was auld, and ze hae gat mair,
   Sum other dule ze drie, O.
O, I hae killed my fadir deir,
     Mither, mither:
O, I hae killed my fadir deir,
   Alas! and wae is mee, O.

[IV.]
And quhatten penance will ze drie for that,

Edward, Edward?
And quhatten penance will ze drie for that?
My deir son, now tell me, O.
Ile set my feit in zonder boat,
Mither, mither:
Ile set my feit in zonder boat,
And Ile fare ovir the sea, O.

[V.]
And quhat wul ze doe wi' zour towirs and zour ha',
Edward, Edward?
And quhat wul ze doe wi' zour towirs and zour ha',
That were sae fair to see, O?
Ile let thame stand till they doun fa',
Mither, mither:
Ile let thame stand till they doun fa',
For here nevir mair maun I bee, O.

[VI.]
And quhat wul ze leive to zour bairns and zour wife,
Edward, Edward?
And quhat wul ze leive to zour bairns and zour wife,
Quhan ze gang over the sea, O?
The warldis room, let them beg throw life,
Mither, mither:
The warldis room, let them beg throw life,
For thame nevir mair wul I see, O.

[VII.]
And quhat wul ze leive to zour ain mither deir,
Edward, Edward?
And quhat wul ze leive to zour ain mither deir?
My deir son, now tell me, O.
The curse of hell frae me sall ze beir,
Mither, mither:
The curse of hell frae me sall ze beir,
Sic counseils ze gave to me, O.

Edward

[I.]
Dein Schwert, wie ist's von Blut so roth?
        Edward, Edward!
Dein Schwert, wie ist's von Blut so roth,
        Und gehst so traurig her?–O!
O ich hab' geschlagen meinen Geier todt,
        Mutter, Mutter!
O ich hab' geschlagen meinen Geier todt
        Und keinen hab ich wie Er–O!

[II.]
Dein's Geiers Blut ist nicht so roth,
        Edward, Edward!
Dein's Geiers Blut ist nicht so roth,
        Mein Sohn, bekenn mir frei–O!
O ich hab' geschlagen mein Rothroß todt,
        Mutter, Mutter!
O ich hab' geschlagen mein Rothroß todt,
        Und 's war so stolz und treu–O!

[III.]
Dein Roß war alt und hast's nicht noth,
        Edward, Edward!
Dein Roß war alt und hast's nicht noth,
        Dich drückt ein anderer Schmerz–O!
O ich hab' geschlagen meinen Vater todt,
        Mutter, Mutter!
O ich hab' geschlagen meinen Vater todt,
        Und weh, weh ist mein Herz–O!

[IV.]
Und was für Buße willst du nun thun?
        Edward, Edward!
Und was für Buße willst du nun thun?

Mein Sohn, bekenn' mir mehr–O!
Auf Erden soll mein Fuß nicht ruhn,
Mutter, Mutter!
Auf Erden soll mein Fuß nicht ruhn,
Will gehn fern über's Meer–O!

[V.]
Und was soll werden dein Hof und Hall?
Edward, Edward!
Und was soll werden dein Hof und Hall,
So herrlich sonst und schön?–O!
Ich lass' es stehn, bis es sink' und fall',
Mutter, Mutter!
Ich lass' es stehn, bis es sink' und fall',
Mag nie es wieder sehn–O!

[VI.]
Und was soll werden dein Weib und Kind?
Edward, Edward!
Und was soll werden dein Weib und Kind?
Wann du gehst über Meer?–O!
Die Welt ist groß, lass' sie betteln drinn,
Mutter, Mutter!
Die Welt ist groß, lass' sie betteln drinn,
Ich seh' sie nimmermehr–O!

[VII.]
Und was willst du lassen deiner Mutter theu'r?
Edward, Edward!
Und was willst du lassen deiner Mutter theu'r?
Mein Sohn, das sage mir–O!
Fluch will ich euch lassen und höllisch Feu'r,
Mutter, Mutter!
Fluch will ich euch lassen und höllisch Feu'r,
Denn Ihr, Ihr riethet's mir!–O!

Translated by Johann Gottfried von Herder

Édouard, Édouard

[I.]
"Pourquoi le sang dégoutte-t-il de votre épée,
    Édouard, Édouard?
Pourquoi le sang dégoutte-t-il de votre épée,
    Et pourquoi êtes-vous triste, oh?"
"Oh, j'ai tué mon faucon si brave,
    Ma mère, ma mère,
Oh, j'ai tué mon faucon si brave,
    Et n'avais d'autre que lui, oh!"

[II.]
"Votre faucon n'a jamais eu de sang si rouge,
    Édouard, Édouard,
Votre faucon n'a jamais eu de sang si rouge,
    Mon cher fils, je te le dis, oh!"
"Oh, j'ai tué mon cheval rouan,
    Ma mère, ma mère,
Oh, j'ai tué mon cheval rouan,
    Qui était si beau et souple, oh!"

[III.]
"Ce cheval était vieux, et vous avez d'autres,
    Édouard, Édouard,
Ce cheval était vieux, et vous avez d'autres,
    Dites-moi la vérité, oh!"
"Oh, c'est mon père que j'ai tué,
    Ma mère, ma mère,
Oh, c'est mon père que j'ai tué,
    Hélas! et malheur à moi, oh!"

[IV.]
"Quelle pénitence ferez-vous pour cela,
    Édouard, Édouard?
Quelle pénitence ferez-vous pour cela,

Mon cher fils, dites-le-moi, oh!"
"Je monterai sur ce bateau là-bas,
    Ma mère, ma mère,
Je monterai sur ce bateau là-bas
    Et m'en irai par la mer, oh!"

[V.]

"Et vos tours et votre château, qu'en ferez-vous,
    Édouard, Édouard?
Et vos tours et votre château, qu'en ferez-vous,
    Qui étaient si beaux à voir, oh!"
"Qu'ils restent debout, jusqu'à ce qu'ils tombent,
    Ma mère, ma mère,
Qu'ils restent debout, jusqu'à ce qu'ils tombent,
    Car ici jamais ne dois être, oh!"

[VI.]

"Que laissez-vous à vos enfants et votre femme,
    Édouard, Édouard?
Que laissez-vous à vos enfants et votre femme,
    Si vous partez sur la mer, oh?"
"Le monde entier, pour qu'ils mendient toute leur vie,
    Ma mère, ma mère,
Le monde entier, pour qu'ils mendient toute leur vie,
    Car jamais plus les verrai, oh!"

[VII.]

"Et que laissez-vous à votre mère chérie,
    Édouard, Édouard?
Et que laissez-vous à votre mère chérie,
    Mon cher fils, dites-le-moi, oh!"
"Ma malédiction d'enfer sur toi,
    Ma mère, ma mère,
Ma malédiction d'enfer sur toi,
    De tels conseils m'as donnés, oh!"

Translated by Louis Cazamian

   IT IS TRADITIONAL TO TWIT Percy about his spelling. One is meant to suspect him of having "antiqued" it a little. He gives the effect of having discovered an ancient manuscript and of having faithfully copied it out—which was not the case. He includes a note in the fourth edition (1794) of the *Reliques* saying that "Edward, Edward" had been "transmitted" to him by Sir David Dalrymple, Bart., of Hailes. I should have thought that anyone "transmitting" a ballad in the Bishop's day would have recorded it for him with the words spelled more or less as they are usually spelled now, but never mind— I can understand how an antiquarian might find it irresistible to set down the ballad in words spelled as they were, or might have been, spelled when the ballad was new. The fanciful spelling does not affect their pronunciation in any way and, unlike the ticket sellers in the Gare d'Orléans, *we* can still read them.

The human race is inclined to keep its ancient treasures as "ancyent" as possible, and Thomas Percy, Bishop of Dromore, was human above all. Since, apparently, he hasn't meddled with the poem otherwise, I am willing to forgive him his little affectations. And I forgive him for the reason that "behemoth" gives me pleasure, and "hippopotame" gives me none; and I forgive him because I think that if Coleridge had stuck by his original spelling in the title of "The Rhyme of the Ancyent Marinere," his translators would not have dreamt of settling for "Le Vieux Matelot" or "Der Alte Matrose." For their ears he might as well have called his poem "The Old Salt" in the first place.

In any event "Edward, Edward" is one of the most fabulous ballads there is, and both translations are very convincing. Herder, because English is a Germanic language, had little trouble in finding the rhymes. Cazamian, on the other hand, confronted by a much more difficult task, arrived at the very ingenious alternative of clanging out uneven, unexpected, internal rhymes with which he achieves a wonderfully pernicious effect. There must have been a French translation before Professor Cazamian's (1946), but I have not found it. Sight unseen, it can scarcely have been finer than his.

The tune of this ballad is lost. There certainly was one. There were probably more than one. I have never found a trace of such a tune, and not one of my "musicologist" friends remembers ever having seen it. To an ordinary musician "Edward" suggests only Brahms.

"Edward" is the motto of the first Brahms Ballade (op. 10), which is the only one of the Ballades Brahms has given a motto. "Nach der schottischen Ballade: 'Edward' in Herder's 'Stimmen der Völker'" is printed under the title. Brahms does not pretend to follow the rhythm or the rhyme scheme of the poem in his Ballade, as he would have done had he been making a song of it, nor does he attempt any Scottish effects in the music, as some of his contemporaries were doing. Only the dramatic dialogue is suggested. Outside of that the poem serves him only as a kind of program note. Why he wanted this device is probably written down somewhere. I have never looked it up.

In such ballads as "The Ravens" and "Edward" the words came first. They were composed to be sung to improvised music, in baronial halls and at military camps, by the single voice of the bard himself. They are the professional compositions of minstrels and harpers, or of the lyric poet-musicians who came after them; they are not at all by "the people" or "das Volk" or "le peuple."

Not that there have not always been amateur folk minstrels as well (including endless cowboys and hillbillies), but these ballads are not by the likes of them. I cannot believe that "Edward" was ever popular in the sense that "Git along, little dogie" is popular. I don't think delivery boys ever whistled it in the street.

"Yankee Doodle," on the other hand, is a popular tune, but it is not a ballad. "Yankee Doodle" works the other way round.

ANONYMOUS

From **Yankee Doodle**

Yankee Doodle came to town,
  Riding on a pony;
He stuck a feather in his cap
  And called it macaroni.

  Yankee Doodle keep it up,
    Yankee Doodle dandy;
  Mind the music and the step,
    And with the girls be handy.

From **Yankee Doodle**

Ein Yankee Bursch ist fix und schlank
Und niemals überfett, Herr,
Und wo Gelag und Tanz und Gang,
Wie'n Katz so flink und nett, Herr!

  Yankee, acht der Küste gut,
    Yankee doodle dandy,
  Drehn und Prahlen nichts dir thut,
    Yankee doodle dandy!

[Three more stanzas follow.]

Translated by
Edmund Freiherr von Beaulieu-Marconnay

From **Yankee Doodle**

Père et moi partons pour le camp,
"Captain Goodwin" nous laisse;

L'armée était, ah! mes enfants!
Comme un pudding, épaisse.
  Yankee Doodle, tiens-toi bien,
  Yankee Doodle dandy,
  Des pas, de l'air te souviens,
  Avec les girls sois poli!

[Nine more stanzas follow.]

Translated by Ch. Senin

THE TUNE OF "Yankee Doodle" came first. It was the invention of an eighteenth-century American who whistled as he walked. Nobody knows who he was nor where, but it was a good, durable tune he had there, and it was certainly set to no words. It is quite obviously the kind of tune that was never meant to be sung at all—only whistled. Later on, somehow, a fife took over the whistling and a drum was added to the fife and marching feet were added to the beat of the drum. A proper fife tune requires no further accompaniment.

Next it needed a name to distinguish it from other fife tunes. Since "tootling" is a technical term and means "double tonguing" in the shoptalk of flute, piccolo, and fife players—because, I am told, "double tonguing" is accomplished by blowing the word "tootle" into a hole in one of these instruments—this drillground tune *may* have been called "The Yankee Tootle" just at first to distinguish it from other tootles. It was not until later when the words were added that Yankee Doodle was personified as the cocky braggart with the pony and the feather in his cap. Outside of serious fife-playing circles it would not take a word like "tootle" very long to blur down into "doodle." It is a characteristic of English—certainly of American English—to slip a peg.

I am simply contributing my modest, nebulous guess about this to the bottomless grab bag of guesses already well established, from which I am freely cribbing all the bits I can believe in at all. The rest is nonsense.

Won't you have a look at what I have set down here—chronologically—before we go on to considering the translations?

After the tune—and nobody knows just how long after—comes the well-known, semi-legendary, pseudo-historic part about the British physician, Dr. Richard Shuckburgh, sitting on the well curb at Fort Crailo in 1758, watching the militia drilling while he writes his "contemptuous verses" to their marching tune. Sometimes Dr. Shuckburgh is not a doctor at all, but a Dutchman called Shuckburg —Shackburg, even—whose house at Rensselaer, New York, built by the Van Rensselaer family in about 1704, is called "Yankee Doodle House" now and is a historic monument shown to visitors.

Something like my own childhood version, quoted here from *The Oxford Dictionary of Nursery Rhymes,* has become the standard "Yankee Doodle" and is best known of them all. Whether or not this is actually the genuine Fort Crailo original, nobody knows, and I don't believe it matters.

Ten years after 1758, in the Boston *Journal of the Times* for September 29, 1768, the "Yankee Doodle Song" is called "band music," even though "Song" implies that by this time there were words to the tune.

The "early version of the tune . . . given in an American manuscript dated 1775," to which Iona and Peter Opie refer in their dictionary, suggests a recording of the tune without words; but words to a "New Song" to "the tune *Yankey* [*sic*] *Doodle,*" composed shortly after the siege of Quebec by "a gentleman just arrived from Newfoundland," were printed in *The Bath Chronicle* on November 21, 1776. The gentleman responsible for this sour piece of endless doggerel must have been a British gentleman, since the verses are directed against Benedict Arnold, Colonel Greene, and other Revolutionary soldiers.

In 1792 it appeared again in James Aird's *Selection of Scottish, English, Irish, and Foreign Airs for Fife, Violin or German Flute,* published in Glasgow without words. "Virginia Melody" and a "Negro

Jig," both anonymous and both forgotten, are the two other "foreign" airs from America in Aird's collection.

In 1784, in the opera *Two for One* by Samuel Arnold, the tune was sung by a character called Dicky Ditto. Here the first line was "Adzooks, old Crusty, why so rusty?" which I am very sorry to say is the only line of it I can find.

It turns up next in *The Contrast*, a play by Royal Tyler, with music made up of borrowed popular tunes. This opened in New York on April 16, 1787, at the John Street Theatre. Tyler has given the tune four original stanzas of excruciating verse which must have been side-splitting in 1787. The first verse, the only one still vaguely familiar, is the one in which "Captain Goodwin," somehow, rhymes with "hasty pudding." It may be that the character called Yankee Jonathan, who sang these horrible words, pronounced them a little differently from the way they are said now—how did he manage it, I wonder: Goodwin, pudwin? Gooding, pudding? more likely; Goodin', puddin'? most likely—but in spite of these complications this Yankee personage, who was to go through any number of transformations and changes of name and costume over the years before he established himself finally and permanently as "Uncle Sam," was a creation of Royal Tyler's. In this play Yankee Jonathan says that he himself knows only 180 verses of this tune, but "our Tabitha at home can sing it all." Tyler was a member of the class of 1776 at Harvard and a classmate of John Trumbull, who painted a portrait of him which has disappeared from everything but Trumbull's own list of his paintings.

A version for 1788 is in Charles Dibdin's *Musical Tour*, and here the first line is "I sing Ulysses and those chiefs."

This play is followed by another play—and a very popular one it must have been—in which the tune turns up yet again with still another set of words. This play, *The Glory of Columbia, Her Yeomen*, by William Dunlap, opened in New York at the Park Theatre on the Fourth of July, 1803, and was performed at intervals and in various places for many years. Its last recorded performance was in 1847. Forty-four years is a long run.

In 1876 *Yankee Doodle*—this time neither a tune nor words, but a painting of the tune—by Archibald Willard of Ohio was exhibited at the Philadelphia Centennial Exposition to thousands of visitors. The idea had burst into favor again and the painting was an overwhelming patriotic success. During the summer it had become so popular that, after the Exposition closed, it was taken on tour and shown in many cities all over the United States. In Boston, when it was being shown there, there was a familiar figure, a kind of half-wit-about-town who sold newspapers, known to his friends as Yankee Doodle. Expecting to see a portrait of him, so many of his friends were disappointed that the name of the picture was changed to *The Spirit of '76*, which it has been called ever since.

The first stanzas in both the German translations I have seen are translations of Dunlap's first stanza:

> A Yankee boy is trim and tall,
>   And never over fat, Sir,
> At dance and frolic, hop and ball
>   He's nimble as a gnat, Sir.

This is Dunlap's, and here is Edmund Freiherr von Beauleau-Marconnay's translation of it:

> Ein Yankee Bursch ist fix und schlank
>   Und niemals überfett, Herr,
> Und wo Gelag und Tanz und Gang,
>   Wie'n Katz so flink und nett, Herr!

In German, "gnat" for syllabic reasons becomes "cat," which is nimble enough to do nicely. It is in the German chorus that a curious thing turns up. Something new has been introduced into both translations, the source of which I have been unable to trace to any English version at all. This is Dunlap's innocuous, good-natured chorus:

> Yankee Doodle! Fire away!
>   What Yankee boy's afraid, Sir?
> Yankee Doodle was the tune
>   At Lexington was played, Sir.

Here is the Baron's chorus:

Yankee, acht der Küste gut,
   Yankee doodle dandy,
Drehn und Prahlen nichts dir thut,
   Yankee doodle dandy!

The second German translation, which is hopelessly poor and whose author is nameless, appears in an anthology of translations collected by Hans Grabow in 1886, called *Die Lieder aller Völker und Zeiten*. Here the first line of the chorus is "Yankee Doodle, schütz dein Ufer," which has the same origin—I have never found it, whatever it is—as "Yankee acht die Küste gut," the one given here. I have no clue to the dates of these, nor have I any notion of what the popular German attitude was toward the War of 1812, but both German versions are obviously translations of the same thing—even though Grabow claims that his is the one by Dr. Shackburg himself, which, of course, it isn't. Grabow has concentrated the rest of his puzzle-headed mistakes on this subject in one benighted footnote:

> Man thut dem Liede Unrecht, wenn man es, wie oft geschehen, als ein sinnloses Geschwätz bezeichnet; es ist vielmehr ein für den amerikanischen Nationalsinn sehr charakteristisches keckes Trutzlied voll Originalität.

Come, come, Herr Grabow! I am afraid the whole point of this has completely escaped you. Yankee Doodle *is* a nonsense song, in spite of what you say, and of course the words are "sinnloses Geschwätz." That is exactly what they are above all. It is "keck"—I will be the first to grant you that—but it is only in the German versions that it gets to be a "Trutzlied."

The French version is a translation of the Royal Tylor one with a number of unaccountable variations of its own thrown in as the stanzas run along. It has its footnote too, as amusing and just as benighted as the German one is, but in another way:

L'expression "Yankee Doodle" n'a pas d'équivalent français; elle peut traduire à peu près "Le Nigaud Américain" ou, mieux, par "Le Dadais Américain."

How's that again? The American booby? The American ninny? The American noodle? Heigho-ho!

As I said—about two hundred years ago—the tune of "Yankee Doodle" came first, and it will always come first.*

---

* A condensed version of part of this commentary appeared in the Sunday magazine section of the St. Louis *Post-Dispatch* for July 1, 1962.

W. H. AUDEN

"Look, stranger, on this island now"

Look, stranger, on this island now
The leaping light for your delight discovers,
Stand stable here
And silent be,
That through the channels of the ear
May wander like a river
The swaying sound of the sea.

Here at the small field's ending pause
When the chalk wall falls to the foam and its tall ledges
Oppose the pluck
And knock of the tide,
And the shingle scrambles after the suck-
ing surf,
And the gull lodges
A moment on its sheer side.

Far off like floating seeds the ships
Diverge on urgent voluntary errands,
And the full view
Indeed may enter
And move in memory as now these clouds do,
That pass the harbor mirror
And all the summer through the water saunter.

Regarde, étranger

Regarde, étranger, vers cette île
Que la lumière bondissante révèle pour ton délice.
Demeure immobile

Et fais silence,
Qu'aux détours de ton oreille
Puisse serpenter comme un fleuve
La rumeur onduleuse des eaux.

Ici où s'arrête comme en suspens ce petit champ,
Où le mur de craie s'abat vers l'écume résistant
De son haut rebord à l'arrachement
Et aux coups de la marée,
Où le gelet s'agrippe au flux qui l'aspire
Tandis qu'une mouette se pose
Un moment sur son flanc pur.

Au loin comme des graines flottantes les vaisseaux
S'écartent pour des courses aux pressants desseins
Et tout ce que l'on voit
Oui tout cela peut entrer
Et bouger dans la mémoire comme font ces nuages
Qui passent sur le miroir du port
Et flânent tout l'été parmi les eaux.

Translated by Claudine Chonez

Sieh, Fremder, diese Insel an

Sieh, Fremder, diese Insel an
Die springendes Licht für deine Lust entdeckt,
Hier stehe fest
Und schweige still,
Das durch des Ohres Rinnen mag,
Wie ein Fluß sich wandern lässt,
Der schwingender Meereslaut.

Pausiere hier an Feldchens Endung
Wenn die Kreidewand zum Schaum fällt und die Riffe
Wiederstehen den Hauch

Und das Klopfen der Flut,
Das Gerölle klettert hinaus, der sau-
gende Brandung
Nach, und die Möwe
Nimmt sich am Felsen Hut.

Weit fort, wie schwimmende Samen, weichen
Die Schiffe sich ab in drängend, freiwillige Botschaften.
Der volle Blick
Dürft freilich hinein
Ins Gedächtniss kommen und da sich rühren wie jetzt diese
    Wolken
Die den Hafenspiegel übergehen
Und den ganzen Sommer durch das Wasser schleudern.

Translated by Victor Proetz

I HAVE CHOSEN "Look, stranger" for a number of reasons: first, I find it more and more wonderful as time goes on; second, Auden liked it well enough to have given two books of verse titles quoted from its first line; third, because, of the four poems of Auden's in G.-A. Astre's *Anthologie de la poésie anglaise contemporaine*, which is all of Auden I have seen in French, I think this one comes through best. The bones of it have kept their shapes, and by bones I mean the extraordinary repeating skeletons of these three stanzas. They have been so delicately hung in space that they suggest three similar cages hanging in a row, to hold three different sets of progressing words to fit the repeating music of Auden's imaginary song.

It is a strenuous and sordid thing to make too thorough-going an analysis of anybody's poetry. This may be why so many translators—who are obliged to do it—come out of their laboratories sounding so tired and dirty. A good translator is in honor bound to leave no stone unturned while his endless weighings and pawings-over of every conceivable linguistic trial and error are in progress. Sometimes in the end, with a pat or two and a little pressing, he can flatten out his translation enough to make it lie again on paper—sometimes not. More often it comes out sounding a little crinkly. The Chonez translation into French is beautiful.

This is the second poem I have ever had the temerity to touch. (Pippa's "Song" was the first.) I was obliged to do it (in my own mind, at least), since there was no translation into German, and I offer my distinguished apologies to Mr. Auden (if not to Mr. Browning, particularly).

I am not altogether dissatisfied with the trick rhyme in the second stanza nor with the last four or five lines in the third one. A word like "Hafenspiegel" is a piece of the purest luck—"potluck," Auden himself calls it—and having luck in German is new to me. I tried this translation partly for the hell of undertaking something too difficult, and partly to get myself into the same questionable boat into which I have been obliged, unavoidably, to put so many other translator fellows. Even though it may be arbitrary for me to be breaking one of my own best tea cups in public just because they have been breaking theirs, I do think it is polite.

JANE AUSTEN

Pride and Prejudice

(From Chapter XVIII)

When supper was over, singing was talked of, and she had the mortification of seeing Mary, after very little entreaty, preparing to oblige the company. By many significant looks and silent entreaties, did she endeavor to prevent such a proof of complaisance,—but in vain; Mary would not understand them; such an opportunity of exhibiting was delightful to her, and she began her song. Elizabeth's eyes were fixed on her with most painful sensations; and she watched her progress through the several stanzas with an impatience which was very ill rewarded at their close; for Mary, on receiving amongst the thanks of the table, the hint of a hope that she might be prevailed on to favour them again, after the pause of half a minute began another. Mary's powers were by no means fitted for such a display; her voice was weak, and her manner affected.—Elizabeth was in agonies. She looked at Jane, to see how she bore it; but Jane was very composedly talking to Bingley. She looked at her two sisters, and saw them making signs of derision at each other, and at Darcy, who continued, however, impenetrably grave. She looked at her father to entreat his interference, lest Mary should be singing all night. He took the hint, and when Mary had finished her second song, said aloud,

"That will do extremely well, child. You have delighted us long enough."

Les cinq filles de Mrs. Bennet

(From Chapter XVIII)

Le souper terminé, on proposa un peu de musique et elle eut l'ennui de voir Mary, qu'on en avait à peine priée, se préparer à charmer l'auditoire. Du regard, elle tenta de l'en dissauder, mais enchantée de cette occasion de se produire, Mary ne voulut pas comprendre et commença une romance. Elizabeth l'écouta chanter plusieurs strophes avec une impatience qui ne s'apaisa point à la fin du morceau; car quelqu'un ayant exprimé vaguement l'espoir de l'entendre encore, Mary se remit au piano. Son talent n'était pas à la hauteur de la circonstance; sa voix manquait d'ampleur et son interprétation de naturel. Elizabeth au supplice lança un coup d'œil à Jane pour savoir ce qu'elle en pensait, mais Jane causait tranquillement avec Bingley. Ses yeux se tournèrent alors vers les deux sœurs qu'elle vit échanger des regards amusés, vers Mr. Darcy, qui gardait le même sérieux impénétrable, vers son père, enfin, à qui elle fit signe d'intervenir, dans la crainte que Mary ne continuât à chanter toute la nuit. Mr. Bennet comprit et lorsque Mary eut achevé son second morceau, il dit à haute voix:

"C'est parfait, mon enfante. Mais vous nous avez charmés assez longtemps."

Translated by V. Leconte and Ch. Pressoin

Stolz und Vorurteil

(From Chapter XVIII)

Als das Essen vorüber war, sprach man von Gesang, und sie sah zu ihrem Kummer, daß Mary auf sehr geringes Bitten hin sich anschickte, die Gesellschaft zu erfreuen. Durch bedeutsame Blicke und schweigendes Flehen suchte sie diesen Gefälligkeitsbewis zu verhindern, doch umsonst. Mary wollte sie nicht verstehen; solch eine Gelegenheit, sich zeigen zu dürfen, war ihr helles Entzücken, und schon begann sie zu singen. Mit peinlichsten Empfindungen heftete Elizabeth ihre Blicke auf sie und folgte dem Ablauf vieler Strophen mit einer Ungeduld, die am Ende schlecht belohnt wurde. Denn Mary, die aus dem

Dank der Gesellschaft den Wunsch heraushörte, sie möge noch etwas zum besten geben, begann nach einer Pause von einer halben Minute mit dem nächsten Lied. Ihre Kräfte reichten keineswegs für solch eine Darbietung aus: die Stimme war schwach und ihr Vortrag geziert. Elizabeth litt Qualen. Sie suchte Jane mit den Augen, um zu sehen, wie sie es ertrug. Aber Jane unterhielt sich friedlich mit Bingley. Sie schaute nach ihren zwei anderen Schwestern aus und bemerket, daß sie sich spöttische Zeichen gaben. Dann sandte sie ihrem Vater flehende Blicke, er möge dem ein Ende setzen, auf daß Mary nicht die ganze Nacht hindurch singe. Er verstand den Wink, und als das zweite Lied beendet war, sagte er laut:

"Nun, das genügt vollkommen, mein Kind. Du hast uns jetzt lange genug erfreut."

Translated by Ilse Krämer

JANE AUSTEN IS HEAVEN in any man's language. Listen to her! How, in French and German, can they keep her and these characters of hers sounding so English?

I have chosen this particular fragment because I think—on no grounds at all—that it must be as familiar to everybody as any other fragment would have been. Besides, I wanted to hear this speech of Mr. Bennet's.

I am by no means a Jane-ite—Jane-ist?—or whatever it is those Austen fanatics call themselves, who go on conducted tours in chara-bancs to Steventon and Bath and Alton to touch things that used to be hers and to brood over locks of her hair. Jane Austen's novels are to me far and away the most enchanting of her memorabilia, and I have most of them right here by my side.

Friends of mine have silenced their children with great success in roomfuls of people merely by murmuring Mr. Bennet's deathless words into their ghastly little ears. It never fails to do the trick, and it is very polite.

Once, in the third class compartment of a French train, a young mother, exasperated with her little chatterbox, stared frankly through the window at the Loire, pretending not to n-o-t-i-c-e anything, while her incorrigible child climbed into my lap, ate a peach, and played with my ears. Had I known enough to say, " '*C'est parfait, mon enfant—mais vous nous avez charmés assez longtemps,*' " I could have been rid of her without even bothering to offend her mother.

IRVING BERLIN

WHEN I WENT TO THE New York Public Library to look for some translations of Irving Berlin they told me, to my great amazement, that there weren't any. Isn't this incredible?

A few days later I decided to try again and to begin at the beginning. I telephoned Mr. Berlin's office and asked to speak to his secretary. She was very much interested to hear what it was I wanted. So far as she knew, nobody had ever inquired about them before. The library was almost, but not quite, right. One piece of Irving Berlin's music had been published both in France and in Germany and that was all. Although they had them both, she had never even seen them herself. At any time I cared to come round to the Irving Berlin Music Corporation she would arrange to have them taken out of the safe for me to look at. I couldn't be permitted to take them away with me, of course, since one copy of each was all they had.

And which one was that? I was hoping for something like "Alexander's Ragtime Band."

"I'm Dreaming of a White Christmas." Imagine that! What a dud! I was bitterly disappointed. "That has never lost its popularity," she said. "Thousands of copies of that are still being sold every year."

I thanked her for her courtesy and told her that I would certainly come around to see her—but not at once, since I didn't actually need the material just yet.

Why wouldn't "Alexander's Ragtime Band" (1911) have been published a dozen times in the last fifty years? And why wouldn't "When that Midnight Choo-choo Leaves for Alabam," and "Look at 'em Doing It," to which Vernon and Irene Castle danced the first time I ever saw them, and the "Piccolino," which has very ingenious words, and is the only thing *Berlin* ever wrote in Latin American imitation of Cole Porter—and, above all, why not "Over There"? In German, it occurred to me on second thought, it would have to be changed to "Over Here," and the translator would probably have been criticized for his un-German activity.

As to the "White Christmas," I am no more curious about what becomes of Mr. Berlin at his most banal than I care about what happens when French and German people come to the end of a perfect day, or about only Who can make a *Baum* or an *arbre*.

Irving Berlin's name was on my very first list of candidates for this book. I have always liked him and I want to have him included here even without illustrations.

WILLIAM BLAKE

The Tiger

Tiger, tiger, burning bright
In the forests of the night,
What immortal hand or eye
Could frame thy fearful symmetry?

In what distant deeps or skies
Burnt the fire of thine eyes?
On what wings dare he aspire?
What the hand dare seize the fire?

And what shoulder and what art
Could twist the sinews of thy heart?
And, when thy heart began to beat,
What dread hand and what dread feet?

What the hammer? What the chain?
In what furnace was thy brain?
What the anvil? What dread grasp
Dare its deadly terrors clasp?

When the stars threw down their spears,
And water'd heaven with their tears,
Did He smile His work to see?
Did He who made the lamb make thee?

Tiger, tiger, burning bright
In the forests of the night,
What immortal hand or eye,
Dare frame thy fearful symmetry?

Der Tiger

Tiger, Tiger, lohendes Licht,
Das durch die Nacht der Wälder bricht.
Welches Auge, welche unsterbliche Hand
Hat dich furchtbar in dein Ebenmaß gebannt?

Welche Höhen, welche Tiefen kennt
Das Feuer, das in deinen Augen brennt?
Welche Flügel mögen ihm gebühren?
Welche Hand wagt an den Brand zu rühren?

Welche Macht vermag die Sehnen
Deines Herzens zu zerdehnen?
Schlägt's erst, wie geduckt zum Satze
Krümmt zum Griff sich schon die Tatze.

Welcher Ambos, welcher Hammer war am Werke,
Dein Gehirn zu schmieden, deine Stärke?
Wer kann, angepackt von diesen Fängen,
Deine tödliche Umarmung sprengen?

Als die Sterne ihre Pfeile niedersenkten
Und den Himmel mit ihren Tränen tränkten,
Freute ER, da ER sein Werk erschaute, sich?
Schuf ER, der das Lamm erschuf, auch dich?

Tiger, Tiger, lohendes Licht,
Das durch die Nacht der Wälder bricht.
Welches Auge, welche unsterbliche Hand
Hat dich furchtbar in dein Ebenmaß gebannt?

Translated by Mela Hartwig

L'Énigme

[I.]

O tigre, tigre flamboyant d'ardeur,
Chassant dans les forêts de la nuit;
Quel pouvoir immortel, inouï,
Modela ta forme de terreur?

[II.]

De quel ciel, de quelle profondeur
Vient ce feu qui dans tes yeux scintille?
Comment donc a-t-on pu le saisir
Et le communiquer à ton coeur?

[III.]

Quelle puissance, quelle volonté,
Pourraient nouer ton coeur prodigieux?
En naissant, monstrueuse entité,
Tes griffes, tes crocs, firent peur!

[IV.]

Avec quel marteau t'a-t-on forgé?
Et ton cerveau, où fut-il trempé?
Sur quelle enclume? . . . Par quelle main
Desserre-t-on ta mortelle étreinte?

[V.]

Quand les étoiles au ciel sourirent
Et mouillèrent l'Eden de leurs pleurs,
De voir Son oeuvre, prit-Il plaisir,
Lui qui créa l'agneau de douceur?

[VI.]

O tigre, tigre flamboyant d'ardeur,
Chassant dans les forêts de la nuit;
Quel pouvoir immortel, inouï,
Modela ta forme de terreur?

*Translated by Félix Rose**

* In 1969 the translator corrected and slightly revised his published translation; these changes have been incorporated here. *Ed.*

Le Tigre

Tigre, tigre, brûlant éclair
Dans les forêts de la nuit,
Quel œil, quelle main immortelle
A pu ordonner ta terrifiante symétrie?

Dans quelles profondeurs lointaines, dans quels cieux
Brûlait le feu de tes yeux?
Sur quelles ailes ose-t-il dresser?
Quelle main osa saisir ce feu?

Et quelle épaule et quel art
Put tordre les muscles de ton cœur?
Et quand ton cœur commença à battre,
Quelle terrible main, quels terrible pieds?

Quel fut marteau, quelle fut la chaîne?
Dans quelle fournaise était ta cervelle?
Quelle fut l'enclume? Quel terrible pouvoir
Osa en étouffer les mortelles terreurs?

Quand les étoiles jetèrent leurs lances
Et abreuvèrent le ciel de leurs larmes,
Sourit-il en contemplant son œuvre?
Celui qui créa l'agneau te créa-t-il?

Tigre, tigre, brûlant éclair
Dans les forêts de la nuit,
Quel œil, quelle immortelle main
Ose ordonner ta terrifiante symétrie?

Translated by M. L. and Philippe Soupault

ONCE, AT HOME FOR THE Christmas holidays, while I was at college, I stood before my mother's looking glass tying a white tie. My mother's room overlooked the street, and hers was the only mirror in the house that had a light at either side of it. I was dressing for a Christmas Eve party and, in the midst of the tying of the tie, some children in the snow, with lighted candles in their hands, began to sing "God rest ye merry, gentlemen," and I was suddenly, unexpectedly dismayed. I was in tears—which is unseemly, God knows, in a man of nineteen. What was worse, I saw myself in the mirror.

"Tiger, tiger" moves me in the same way. I have never managed not to choke a little over the fifth stanza, which I think is one of the Wonders of the World.

Later, when I saw the Blake drawings at the Tate Gallery for the first time, I cracked up again in front of the one called "The Tree Full of Angels." That was the day when my interest in Blake changed from the poems to the drawings. The same summer, at a book stall on the Quai Voltaire, my friend George Howland Butler found an old, battered copy of Blair's *Grave* with the Blake illustrations, for which he paid "nothing." I envied him this book so much and so relentlessly that he gave it to me. These engravings, to which I am very much attached, still hang in my sitting room—but now, years later, somehow I find myself softly changing back to the poems again, and I don't know why.

In "Tiger, tiger" every line of Blake's is precisely four feet long. This never varies and, because of it, the German translation must have been a fearful struggle. Although the rhyme scheme has been made to work—forced to work, I almost said—the lines get to be four, five, and even six feet long, and come through, almost completely out of hand, in a very informal arrangement and in quite another meter—if any. And this is nobody's fault! It must have been very difficult indeed for the German translator to make up her mind just when her translation was ready to be read—to say nothing of printed. But, in spite of her misgivings,

> Als die Sterne ihre Pfeile niedersenkten
> Und den Himmel mit ihren Tränen tränkten

is wonderful enough to have made the game worth all the candles.

Friends of mine have heard Tinker of Yale shout this poem out as he paced up and down the classroom floor. They have never got over it.

In the first French version the poem sounds as though it had been written by using Blake only for notes. It seems not altogether hopeless as a French poem, although I don't think that a French person reading it could be expected to burst into tears, nor do I believe that he would quite understand why anybody would be pacing up and down anywhere shouting it out.

The second version, which I discovered years later, is much, much better. Here are both of them set up side by side for study. I find it very interesting to compare not only the reaction of two Frenchmen to the English language and to Blake, but to compare two unevenly matched translators with each other.

RUPERT BROOKE

The Soldier

If I should die, think only this of me:
   That there's some corner of a foreign field
That is forever England. There shall be
   In that rich earth a richer dust concealed;
A dust whom England bore, shaped, made aware,
   Gave, once, her flowers to love, her ways to roam,
A body of England's, breathing English air,
   Washed by the rivers, blest by the suns of home.

And think, this heart, all evil shed away,
   A pulse in the eternal mind, no less
      Gives somewhere back the thoughts by England given;
Her sights and sounds; dreams happy as her day;
   And laughter, learnt of friends; and gentleness,
      In hearts at peace, under an English heaven.

Der Soldat

Sollte ich sterben, denkt nur dies von mir:
Daß da ein Winkel ist auf fremdem Feld,
Der England ist für immer. Es wird hier
Der reichen Erde reicherer Staub gesellt.

Ein Staub, den England formte, trug, erzog,
Dem England Blumen gab und Wanderzeit,
Ein Stück von ihm, das Englands Lüfte sog,
Von seinen Wassern, seinem Licht geweiht.

Und denkt, dies Herz, das mit erlöstem Schlag
Im Ewigen schlägt, erwidert noch und wahrt,

Was ihm von England kam: Gedank und Stimme;

Und Traum, der glücklich ist wie Englands Tag;
Lachen, das Freunde lehrten; sanfte Art
Friedlicher Herzen unter Englands Himmel.

Translated by Bernt von Heiseler

Le Soldat

Si je meurs, pense seulement
Qu'il existe un carré dans un champ étranger
Qui sera d'Angleterre à jamais. Là-bas,
Dans cette terre riche, une poussière
Plus riche encor demeurera cachée.

L'Angleterre la pétrit, la façonna de corps
Et la forgea d'esprit,
Et lui donna jadis ses fleurs pour les aimer,
Ses routes à parcourir.
C'est le corps d'un anglais, respirant l'air ancestral,
Baigné de ses fleuves, et béni des rayons de son
                                          soleil natal.
Et pense aussi: ce cœur, d'où s'éffaça le mal,
Battement dans l'âme éternelle, ne redonnera pas moins
A ce carré d'un champ les pensées reçues de son pays,
Ses paysages et ses chants; rêves heureux comme sa lumière,
Et les rires, appris de ses amis; sa douceur
Dans les cœurs en paix, et sous de cieux anglais.

Translated by Henri-Marcel and Michel Bernfeld

RUPERT BROOKE'S THIRD SONNET, called "The Dead," and his fifth one—the one here—are established in English now as the two top-ranking survivals of the First War poetry. The opening sentence rises in a long crescendo up, up to "England." This poem by an English soldier is related in spirit and in a number of other ways to the King's Saint Crispin's Day speech in *Henry V*.

What can have happened to the translators here? All three of them have fluffed their lines. Wouldn't, for instance, the German translation have been immeasurably improved by changing the first part of the third line to "Der ist für immer England"? How can this possibly have been overlooked?

Brooke was presented to the French in 1918 for the first time in the most unfortunate way, with translations in prose of a few of his poems. These are in an article about his death, by Jean Dornis, which appeared in Tome XLIII (p. 147) of the *Revue des Deux Mondes*. Who in all of France, I wonder, could have been interested in an outline of anybody's posthumous sonnet in which three little dots take the place of the first three lines of the octave, and in which "paysages" is considered sufficient to cover "sights and sounds"? But even in this brutal presentation an attempt has been made to carry over the opening gun. "Si je meurs au loin, croyez qu'il y aura un arpent de terre dans quelque champ étranger qui sera pour toujours l'Angleterre." This is much better than anything the rhymed translation hasn't done.

The German translation is indeed a sonnet—which must have been considered as enough of an achievement in itself to warrant the translator's neglect of almost everything else. The French one, too, cramped by the fourteen-line limit, bursts blithely into seventeen lines, and "overflows the pot" to no advantage.

Another time, when someone else gets round to trying again, perhaps he can manage to make things sound a little more like Rupert Brooke. This time poor Brooke seems almost to have been left out.

ELIZABETH BARRETT BROWNING

Sonnets from the Portuguese

1.

I thought once how Theocritus had sung
Of the sweet years, the dear and wished-for years,
Who each one in a gracious hand appears
To bear a gift for mortals, old or young:
And, as I mused it in his antique tongue,
I saw, in gradual vision through my tears,
The sweet, sad years, the melancholy years,
Those of my own life, who by turns had flung
A shadow across me. Straightway I was 'ware,
So weeping, how a mystic shape did move
Behind me, and drew me backward by the hair;
And a voice said in mastery, while I strove,—
"Guess now who holds thee?"—"Death," I said. But there
The silver answer rang,—"Not Death, but Love."

6.

Go from me. Yet I feel that I shall stand
Henceforward in thy shadow. Nevermore
Alone upon the threshold of my door
Of individual life, I shall command
The uses of my soul, nor lift my hand
Serenely in the sunshine as before,
Without the sense of that which I forbore—
Thy touch upon the palm. The widest land
Doom takes to part us, leaves thy heart in mine
With pulses that beat double. What I do
And what I dream includes thee, as the wine
Must taste of its own grapes. And when I sue
God for myself, He hears that name of thine,
And sees within my eyes the tears of two.

22.

When our two souls stand up erect and strong,
Face to face, silent, drawing nigh and nigher,
Until the lengthening wings break into fire
At either curvèd point,—what bitter wrong
Can the earth do to us, that we should not long
Be here contented? Think! In mounting higher,
The angels would press on us and aspire
To drop some golden orb of perfect song
Into our deep, dear silence. Let us stay
Rather on earth, Belovèd,—where the unfit
Contrarious moods of men recoil away
And isolate pure spirits, and permit
A place to stand and love in for a day,
With darkness and the death-hour rounding it.

Sonette aus dem Portugiesischen

[1.]

Und es geschah mir einst, an Theokrit
zu denken, der von jenen süßen Jahren
gesungen hat und wie sie gütig waren
und gebend und geneigt bei jedem Schritt:

und wie ich saß, antikischem Gedicht
nachsinnend, sah ich durch mein Weinen leise
die süßen Jahre, wie sie sich im Kreise
aufstellten, traurig, diese Verzicht

lichtloser Jahre: meine Jahre. Da
stand plötzlich jemand hinter mir und riß
aus diesem Weinen mich an meinem Haar.

Und eine Stimme rief, die furchtbar war:
"Rate, wer hält dich so?"—"Der Tod gewiß."
"Die Liebe"—klang es wieder, sanft und nah.

[6.]

Geh fort von mir. So werd ich fürderhin
in deinem Schatten steh. Und niemals mehr
die Schwelle alles dessen, was ich bin,
allein betreten. Niemals wie vorher

verfügen meine Seele. Und die Hand
nicht so wie früher in Gelassenheit
aufheben in das Licht der Sonne, seit
die deine drinnen fehlt. Mag Land um Land

anwachsen zwischen uns, so muß doch dein
Herz in dem meinen bleiben, doppelt schlagend.
Und was ich tu und träume, schließt dich ein:

so sind die Trauben überall im Wein.
Und ruf ich Gott zu mir: Er kommt zu zwein
und sieht mein Auge zweier Tränen tragend.

[22.]

Wenn schweigend, Angesicht in Angesicht,
sich unserer Seelen ragende Gestalten
so nahe stehn, daß, nicht mehr zu verhalten,
ihr Feuerschein aus ihren Flügeln bricht:

was tut uns diese Erde dann noch Banges?
Und stiegst du lieber durch die Engel? Kaum;—
sie schütteten uns Sterne des Gesanges
in unsres Schweigens lieben tiefen Raum.

Nein, laß uns besser auf der Erde bleiben,
wo alles Trübe, was die andern treiben,
die Reinen einzeln zueinander hebt.

Da ist gerade Plaz zum Stehn und Lieben
für einen Tag, von Dunkelheit umschwebt
und von der Todesstunde rund umschrieben.

Translated by Ranier Maria Rilke

Sonnets from the Portuguese

I.

Je pensais l'autre jour aux chants de Théocrite
Sur les douces années, chères et bienheureuses,
Dont chacune paraît, en ses mains vigoureuses,
Apporter un présent aux mortels qu'elle invite.

Et comme je rêvais dans sa langue insolite,
Je revis, à travers mes larmes douloureuses,
D'autres années, hélas tristes et rigoureuses,
Dont l'ombre tour à tour voilà ma vie maudite.

Pleurant ainsi, derrière moi je crus sentir
Un spectre qui soudain tenta de me saisir
Par les cheveux. Sa voix, qui semblait un prodige

Demanda, magistrale et tendre tour à tour:
"Devine qui te tient maintenant?"—"La Mort," dis-je.
"Non," dit la voix d'argent. "Pas la Mort, mais l'Amour."

VI.

Eloigne-toi. Pour moi, je vivrai désormais
Dans ton ombre, toujours. Jamais plus, solitaire,
Sur le seuil de ma chambre, jamais, recluse austère,
Je ne serai maîtresse de mon coeur. Jamais

Ma main ne jouira du soleil, de l'air frais,
Sans évoquer le sacrifice volontaire
Que je fis de la joie qui m'était la plus chère:
La douceur de ta main dans la mienne. Je sais

Que le plus vaste espace qu'entre nous placera
Le plus cruel destin, jamais n'empêchera
Ton coeur de battre dans le mien. Tu fais partie

De ma chair, de mon rêve, et lorsque je prie Dieu
C'est ton nom qu'Il entend, comme Il voit dans mes yeux
Les larmes de tes yeux et ta vie dans ma vie.

XXII.

Lorsque nos âmes, cher, se trouvent face à face,
Droites, fortes, silencieuses, se rapprochant
Jusqu'au moment au leurs ailes en se touchant
Font jaillir l'étincelle—alors quelle menace

Peut contenir pour nous cette terre fugace?
Réfléchis bien. Si nous montions aux plus hauts champs
Les anges nous découvriraient, et de leurs chants
Viendraient vite troubler la très douce bonace.

Du silence qui nous est cher. Donc ne t'envole
Pas, Bien-Aimé. Reste à terre où tout l'effort
Absurde, des humains, et leurs conflits, isolent

Les purs esprits, laissant une place bornée
Où chacun peut aimer et vivre sa journée
Encerclé par la nuit et l'heure de la mort.

Translated by André Maurois

A NUMBER OF WOMEN I KNOW—all of them fairly well along now —agree with my godmother, who told me one time that the *Sonnets from the Portuguese* were "poems for ladies." To illustrate the translations, I have been obliged to turn to my lady friends for help. Without them I could never have known which to choose. They knew instinctively. Unanimously they agreed to I, VI, and XXII—and heaven knows why. In the preface to his translation, André Maurois says he chooses XIV, XX, XXVI, XXVIII, XXX, XLI, and XLIV as being the best of them. But he is a man—and he's a Frenchman. Rilke doesn't say.

To me the *Sonnets* are perfectly matched. They share with one another a consistent excellence which I associate with strings of pearls and with certain pieces of music whose excellence is at a very high, very dead level. It is in music that sounds to me as though Ruskin might have written it—in music like *Les Préludes* of Liszt or

the Saint-Saëns *Variations on a Theme of Beethoven's,* for example.
I may be as blindly mistaken about such music as I am about these
sonnets—or about Ruskin, even.

Somehow, in spite of his feeling against them, Maurois was sufficiently drawn to them to see them through. He finds their meta-
phors a little dated, he says. "Trops d'anges pour notre goût, trop de
lyres, trop du torrents de pleurs," he thinks.

When I was a boy the *Sonnets from the Portuguese,* beautifully
bound, were in all ladies' bedrooms. In my godmother's, they were
in watered lilac silk, and the book was a permanent bibelot on her
bedside table, that had to be dusted every day. It was arranged pret-
tily at an angle on top of Amiel's *Journal,* which lay on top of Dosto-
yevsky's *Idiot,* and it frequently had little bouquets of violets or lilies
of the valley standing near it. My mother's was more austere: hers
was in pearl-gray suede.

Alexander Bernus says somewhere that somebody else's German
translations of Mrs. Browning are better than Rilke's. I can't remember whose they are and, anyway, I haven't found them. Rilke,
he thinks, has put too much of himself into them. What a break for
Mrs. Browning! *I* think. So far as immortality in three languages is
concerned, it seems to me that Mrs. Browning has come off very well
indeed, with some colors flying that aren't even hers.

ROBERT BROWNING

Song from **Pippa Passes**

The year's at the spring,
And day's at the morn;
Morning's at seven;
The hill-side's dew pearl'd;
The lark's on the wing;
The snail's on the thorn;
God's in His heaven—
All's right with the world!

Song from **Pippa geht vorüber**

Das Jahr, wenns frühlingt,
und der Tag wird geborn
morgens um sieben,
der Hang, taubeperlt [*sic*],
die Lerche beschwingt,
die Schnecke am Dorn:
Gott in seinem Himmel—
Gut stehts um die Welt!

Translated by Alexander von Bernus

Song from **Pippa passe**

L'année est au printemps;
Le jour est au matin,
Le matin à l'aurore;

Le flanc de la colline est emperlé de rosée;
L'alouette a pris son essor;
L'escargot rampe sur l'aubépine;
Dieu est au ciel . . .
Tout est bien en ce monde!

Translated by Jules Guiraud

SOMEWHERE IN THE BACK OF MY HEAD I have a big room that looks like a school room because it has a blackboard in it.

Q. So you have attempted a German translation yourself?

A. Yes, sir. I haven't been able to find one.

Q. Did you find your little experiment difficult?

A. I don't think so. I don't remember. I did it only as an exercise. It isn't meant to be any good. I did it in Central Park.

After a year of fruitless prowling I had begun to think that I might be called on to recite one day by whoever it was up there behind the desk. It may have been Mr. Browning himself for all I know.

Q. How did you go about it? What did you do first?

A. Looked up the music.

Q. Why the music?

A. Since this was a song, I wanted to make a translation to fit the music. Reading the French translation may have given me the idea.

Q. It seems a reasonable approach. Did you have any luck?

A. Not the kind I had hoped to have. I wanted Miss Flower's original tune, of course, but maybe she never got round to writing it.

Q. Who is Miss Flower?

A. "We" don't know. "We learn from a letter to Miss Flower that . . . Browning had shown *Pippa* to her, for . . . he wrote suggesting that she compose music for the lyrics," is all "we" know. One of your biographers—I mean to say, one of Mr. Browning's biographers— wrote that. And that's the end of Miss Flower. She doesn't even turn up in the index. Of course I found four other tunes, all of them written in the United States after 1898, for the use of Browning

Societies, I imagine. Anyway, they are all by American ladies and
gentlemen.

Q. By what?

A. By Mrs. H. H. A. Beach, by Miss Natalie Curtis, by Mr. Henry
Kimball Hadley, and by Mr. Harvey Worthington Loomis. Did you
ever hear of these tunes?

Q. No, no—but then, they were all after my time. Tell me this:
What do you consider the *point* of the little poem, and where do you
think it lies?

A. In the last two lines. They must be preserved at any cost.

Q. Why do you think that?

A. Because they are the motto of the play.

Q. Ah! So you have read the play?

A. Yes, just the other day—but frankly only part of it. Just enough
to find that out.

Q. Why did you read it at all?

A. I considered doing it "conscientious." Besides, none of my
friends could help me out. Nobody I telephoned had ever read it.

Q. Never mind, never mind. Now this: Were you convinced
enough of the importance of the last two lines to translate them first
with the idea of studying the other characteristic devices in the little
poem later on, so that if—shall we say—you found His Satanic
Majesty taking the hindmost, he wouldn't be taking your two last
lines away from you?

A. Yes. And besides, I am convinced that even Mr. Browning wrote
them first of all and filled in the snails and larks and things afterwards.

Q. How have you translated the lines? Will you write them on
your mental blackboard for us?

> *Gott ist im Himmel—*
> *Ganz gut geht's der Welt!*

Q. Why?

A. Because the lines contain two phrases that translate themselves
naturally into acceptable, everyday German without being pushed
around at all. They have to do with exactly what I meant a few pages
ago when I wrote that bit about contriving means of getting through
the barriers into the *style* of the second language.

Q. Yes, yes, of course. Hm! What did you do next?

A. Examined the rhyme scheme, I suppose.

Q. Did you consider it important?

A. I considered the two *d*-rhymes very important. The *a-b-c* ones have so much time and so many other rhymes going on in between them that they could almost be ignored or at least partly smothered in the music—if there is any music.

Q. I would be interested to hear what you have done with "dew-pearl'd."

A. I've thrown it out.

Q. Indeed!

A. And that for four reasons—every one of them perfect: the word would have had to be coined over again in German; it is a word that embarrasses me; it was dragged in in the first place only to provide a rhyme anticipating "world," which we don't need here—we need one to anticipate "Welt"; and fourth, it would get to be "thaubeperlt," which is a word I couldn't agree to use.

Q. Why not?

A. It has a very unfortunate sound. It would not be immediately apparent to any one hearing it whether the word was meant to be "thau-beperlt," which is one thing, or "taube-perlt," which is quite another. It's a booby-trap word with a pigeon in it.

Q. Would an educated German person with his German ear and his mind on the poem ever hear the hidden pigeon? Besides, the spelling . . .

A. He wouldn't hear the spelling, and I, for instance, wouldn't like to take a chance.

Q. Were I to say something about "a basinful of water," would you have noticed with your English-tempered ear, that I had said the word "sinful" among other things?

A. I'm not sure. Besides, I may be carping a little. In any event, since it doesn't rhyme with "Welt" at all, we couldn't be using it anyway.

Q. What does rhyme?

A. "Feld." And thank God that isn't too bad. Anytime any dew is pearling a hillside it is probably pearling a field as well. As an image

I think a field is just as poetic as a hillside and just as good-looking and, for practical reasons, "Feld" has only one syllable. I was quite willing to settle for it.

Q. What other characteristics did you notice that you considered indispensable? And I think this is the last question.

A. That in spite of the punctuation, the song is made up of what amounts to eight simple declarative sentences each with the same verb, which Browning repeats eight times.

Q. And what is it?

A. Apostrophes.

Q. Yes, yes, yes—and very amusing it is of the poet, is it not?

A. Amusing? Browning amusing? I think I have never heard that word associated with him before. Isn't it disrespectful?

Q. Never mind. What else is there to be considered?

A. I shouldn't think anything.

Q. So what do you get? Let's have it.

A. *Das Jahr ist am Frühling,*
    Der Tag's neugebor'n;
    S'ist Morgens um sieben;
    Thau 'perlet das Feld;
    Die Lerch' ist am Flügel;
    Die Schneck' ist am Dorn;
    Gott ist im Himmel—
    Ganz gut geht's der Welt!

Q. Dear, dear! "Tag's"? "S'ist"? "Lerch' "? "Schneck' "? Really? Don't you object to this kind of hillbilly German?

A. Yes, naturally, sir, *I* do, but Germans don't. German poets do it all the time. Besides, Pippa was a peasant—I just found that out.

Q. And how, since you object so seriously to the pigeon in the fourth line, can you bear the sound of a goose in the last?

A. Now *you're* carping, sir.

What has become of all the Browning Societies everybody's aunts used to belong to, where ladies in feather boas gathered on first and third Thursdays for Browning and tea and cake? Have they all melted away? Are the Brownings out of fashion? Have the Browning Societies become Ogden Nash Societies with martinis and Nash and little sausages stuck with toothpicks? It's a good idea, certainly, but if they have, I haven't heard of it.

At last, luckily, I have found the actual official translation into German of this song of Pippa's, which has been eluding me for so long. Naturally it takes its proper place in the text.

And, incidentally, I have discovered that "souriant, l'enfant tomba mort," and "lächeln, fiel der Knab' zum Tode," are "smiling the boy fell dead."

ROBERT BURNS

Auld Lang Syne

For auld lang syne, my dear,
  For auld lang syne,
We'll tak a cup o' kindness yet
  For auld lang syne.

I.
Should auld acquaintance be forgot,
  And never brought to mind?
Should auld acquaintance be forgot,
  And auld lang syne!

II.
And surely ye'll be your pint-stowp,
  And surely I'll be mine,
And we'll tak a cup o' kindness yet
  For auld lang syne!

III.
We twa hae run about the braes,
  And pou'd the gowans fine,
But we've wander'd monie a weary fit
  Sin' auld lang syne!

IV.
We twa hae paidl'd in the burn
  Frae morning sun till dine,
But seas between us braid hae roar'd
  Sin' auld lang syne.

V.
And there's a hand, my trusty fiere,
  And gie's a hand o' thine,

And we'll tak a right quid willie-waught
   For auld lang syne!

CHORUS
For auld lang syne, my dear,
   For auld lang syne,
We'll tak a cup o' kindness yet
   For auld lang syne!

Le vieux et bon pays

REFRAIN
Au vieux et bon pays, mon cher,
   Au vieux et bon pays,
Nous cliquerons gaîment nos verres
   Au vieux et bon pays.

[I.]
De vieux copains oublieront-ils
   Leur camaraderie?
De vieux copains s'oublieront-ils
   Et le bon vieux pays?

[II.]
Pour sûr, tu me tendras mon verre,
   Voici le tien empli.
Et nous trinquerons sans manière
   Au vieux et bon pays.

[III.]
Nous avons couru la montagne,
   Des fleurs avons cueilli,
N'avons nous pas souffert depuis
   Loin du bon vieux pays?

[IV.]
Sur le lac, de l'aube à la nuit,
   Tous deux avons ramé . . .

L'océan nous a séparés
   Et du bon vieux pays.

[V.]

Prends donc ma main, mon brave ami,
   Donne la tienne aussi.
Tous deux poussons le même cri;
   Au vieux et bon pays!

REFRAIN

Au vieux et bon pays, mon cher,
   Au vieux et bon pays,
Nous cliquerons gaîment nos verres
   Au vieux et bon pays.

*Translated by Félix Rose**

---

* In 1969 the translator corrected and slightly revised his published translation; these changes have been incorporated here. *Ed.*

Lang' lang' ist's her

I.

Und sollten alter Freundschaft wir
Gedenken nimmermehr?
Gedenken alter Freundschaft nicht?
Lang', lang' ist's her.

CHOR.   Lang', lang' ist's her, mein Schatz,
            Lang', lang' ist's her,
            Drum trinken wir vom Herzen eins.
            Lang', lang' ist's her.

II.

Dein Masskrug, der bleibt nimmer voll,
Und rasch wird meiner leer,
Wir trinken recht vom Herzen eins,
Lang', lang' ist's her.

III.

Einst rupften wir die Blumen ab
Und rannten kreuz und quer—
Nun sind die alten Füsse müd',
Lang', lang' ist's her.

IV.

Einst patschten wir durch Pfütz' und Bach,
Hei, das gefiel uns sehr!
Dann brausten Meere zwischen uns—
Lang', lang' ist's her.

V.

Reich mir die Hand, mein alter Freund,
Nun lass' ich dich nicht mehr!
Wir trinken heute herzhaft eins,
Lang', lang' ist's her.

Translated by Edmund Ruete

IN A LETTER DATED 17th December, 1788, Robert Burns wrote to Mrs. Dunlop of Dunlop: ". . . is not the Scotch phrase, 'auld lang syne,' exceedingly expressive? There is an old song and tune which has often thrilled through my soul. You know I am an enthusiast in old Scotch songs. I shall give you the verses on the other sheet." The other sheet is not included in Burns's letters, but I think this is the first verse of what was written there:

Should old acquaintance be forgot,
    And never thought upon,
The flames of love extinguishéd
    And freely past and gone?

with "auld lang syne," and so on, as the refrain.

This is the first stanza of the first recorded version of "Auld Lang Syne," which appeared in 1716—seventy-two years before Burns wrote the letter—in Vol. III of Watson's *Scots Poems*, and it is certainly upon this that Burns's rewritten version is based.

In the letter he speaks of "an old song and tune." Watson's *Scots Poems* is not available, but its title does not suggest a book of songs.

Another version was published between 1724 and 1727—only about eight years after Watson's—by Allan Ramsay in his *Tea-Table Miscellany*. Although this is a collection of Scots and English songs, here again the words are published without the tunes.

> Should auld acquaintance be forgot
>   Though they return with scars?
> These are the noble hero's lot
>   Obtain'd in glorious wars,

is Ramsey's version, which Burns disregards, if he ever heard of it.

Burns's revision, which he lengthened with additional stanzas, was not published until ten years after he wrote the letter to Mrs. Dunlop. It appeared first in 1798 in the first volume of Thomson's *Original Scottish Airs*. This *was* a book of music and in it Burns's verses have been set to the "old song and tune" he speaks of in the letter. This, however, is not our present tune. Thomson's collection was published again the following year, and it was in Thomson's second edition, in 1799, that "Auld Lang Syne" appears for the first time with the tune to which we sing it now.

This second tune—our tune—was not written to these words. It is only another of those serviceable, heavy-duty Scottish airs which, like "Yankee Doodle," came into being while nobody was listening. It had been appearing off and on, in fact, since at least 1757 in various collections of songs when Thomson took it over, and by the time he did, it had already been called "The Miller's Wedding," "The Miller's Daughter," "I Fee's a Lad at Michaelmas," and "Sir Alexander Don's Strathspey," and used, in 1783, in *Rosina*, a play by William Shield, where the music was marked "to imitate the bagpipes."

"Auld lang syne" is a catch phrase—sentimental, nostalgic, and "exceedingly expressive." "Auld" means "old," "lang" means "long," and "syne" means "since" or "ago." Pulled apart these words are nothing, but the phrase is contagious and Burns's verses have been irresistible to endless translators. In spite of the stumbling block which is, of course, the phrase itself, it has been translated into every imaginable language and into French and German half a dozen times. I think I have chosen the best translations.

An enthusiastic young woman I know—girl, actually—thought when she first read them that both these translations were equally good. So did I. After we had sung them together a few times, just to see how well they fitted the tune, she was more enthusiastic still. I was less.

"Can you imagine crowds of people," she said, "singing these on a New Year's Eve in the Place de la Bastille and on the Kurfürstendamm, or whatever the Times Square of Berlin is nowadays?"

"No," I said, "can you?"

I have never been at either of them on a New Year's Eve nor, for that matter, have I ever been to Times Square. Neither has she.

I can—by inconveniencing my imagination a little—almost hear the German version sung as a jolly *Bierstubenlied* (*in Schottischer Weise*) by some of those beery young *Kameraden* you find in German university towns, but I can't for the life of me think of its being sung by any Frenchmen at all. Can you imagine a chain of Frenchmen doing that thing you are meant to do with your arms?

ROBERT BURNS

To a Mouse

On turning her up in her nest
with the plough, November 1785.

I.

Wee, sleekit, cowrin, tim'rous beastie,
O, what a panic's in thy breastie!
Thou need na start awa sae hasty
      Wi' bickering brattle!
I wad be laith to rin an' chase thee,
      Wi' murdering pattle!

II.

I'm truly sorry man's dominion
Has broken Nature's social union,
An' justifies that ill opinion
      Which makes thee startle
At me, thy poor, earth-born companion
      An' fellow mortal!

III.

I doubt na, whyles, but thou may thieve;
What then? poor beastie, thou maun live!
A daimen icker in a thrave
      'S a sma' request;
I'll get a blessin wi' the lave,
      An' never miss 't!

IV.

Thy wee-bit housie, too, in ruin!
Its silly wa's the win's are strewin!
An' naething, now, to big a new ane,
      O' foggage green!
An' bleak December's win's ensuin,
      Baith snell an' keen!

V.

Thou saw the fields laid bare an' waste,
An' weary winter comin fast,
An' cozie here, beneath the blast,
      Thou thought to dwell,
Till crash! the cruel coulter past
      Out thro' thy cell.

VI.

That wee bit heap o' leaves an' stubble,
Has cost thee monie a weary nibble!
Now thou's turned out, for a' thy trouble,
      But house or hald,
To thole the winter's sleety dribble,
      An' cranreuch cauld!

VII.

But Mousie, thou art no thy lane,
In proving foresight may be vain:
The best-laid schemes o' mice an' men
      Gang aft agley,
An' lea'e us nought but grief an' pain,
      For promis'd joy!

VIII.

Still thou art blest, compared wi' me!
The present only toucheth thee:
But och! I backward cast my e'e,
      On prospects drear!
An' forward, tho' I canna see,
      I guess an' fear!

An eine Maus

[I.]

Du schüchtern, kleines, schlankes Thier,
Mit welcher Angst fliehst Du von hier,

Du brauchst vor meiner Pflugschar Dich
    Ja nicht zu scheun.
Thät' ich Dir weh, es würde mich
    Gar sehr gereuen.

   [II.]
Wie oft zerreißt des Menschen Hand
Der Schöpfung brüderliches Band;
Zur Flucht vor mir hast Du ein Recht,
    Mein kleines Thier;
Aus staubgeborenem Geschlecht
    Bin ich gleich Dir.

   [III.]
Ein kleiner Diebstahl ist Gebrauch
Bei Euch, denn leben müsst ihr auch;
Der Raub vom öden Stoppelfeld
    War ja nur klein,
Wenn Gott das andre mit erhält,
    So mag's drum sein!

   [IV.]
Zertrümmert liegt Dein Häuslein dort;
Was blieb, das treibt der Sturm nun fort,
Du hast, um Dir es neu zu bau'n,
    Nicht Moos, noch Gras,
Und Dein harrt des Dezembers Graun,
    So kalt und naß.

   [V.]
Du sahst, wie öde das Gefeld,
Der Winter nahte rauh und wild,
Du glaubtest, hier im Nest genug
    Geschützt zu sein.
Da krach! brach ich mit meinem Pflug
    Auf dich herein.

   [VI.]
Geknuspert hast Du Tag und Nacht
Am Stroh, und Dir Dein Bett gemacht,

Und dafür treib ich jetzt Dich fort
    Von Hof und Haus,
In's öde Feld, durchstürmt vom Nord,
    Mußt Du hinaus.

[VII.]
Doch, Mäuschen, Du zeigst nicht allein,
Daß Vorsicht kann vergeblich sein,
Der beste Plan von Maus und Mann
    Gelingt oft nicht,
Und Leid und Kummer bringt uns dann,
    Was Lust verspricht.

[VIII.]
Nur bist Du glücklicher als ich,
Das heut allein bekümmert Dich,
Ich, wend' ich rückwärts mein Gesicht,
    Find, ach, nur Schmerz,
Und seh ich auch die Zukunft nicht,
    Bangt doch mein Herz!

Translated by Adolf Laun

An eine Maus

(*Die er mit ihrem Neste aufgepflügt hatte*)

I.
Klein, furchtsam Tierchen, welch ein Schrecken
Erfüllt dein Brüstchen, so durch Hecken
Und Furchen dich zum Lauf zu strecken?
    Bleib! Nicht so jach!
Nicht setz ich mit dem Pflügerstecken
    Grausam dir nach!

II.
Der Mensch—betrübt gesteh ichs ein—
Brach der Natur geselligen Reihn!

Mißtrauisch drum fliehst du feldein,
  Voll Furcht, dir schade
Dein armer Mitgeschaffner—dein
  Staubkamerade!

III.

Mag sein, du gehst auf Diebstahl aus;
Gut! mußt ja leben, kleine Maus!
Manchmal vom Schock ein Ährchen kraus
  Ist klein Begehren!
Der Rest bringst Segen mir ins Haus—
  Ich kann's entbehren!

IV.

Dein klein, arm Häuschen auch zerstört!
Sein töricht Dach der Sturm durchfährt!
Und nirgend Grün mehr, neuen Herd
  Dir zu begründen,
Da Christtag bald die Fluren kehrt
  Mit eisigen Winden!

V.

Du sahst die Felder öde schier,
Den langen Winter vor der Tür
Und sprachst: "Geschützt und kosig hier
  Halt ich es aus!"
Als—Krach!—die böse Pflugschar dir
  Grad fuhr durch's Haus!

VI.

Von Laub und Stroh dein Nestchen klein,
Manch mühsam Knuspern trugs dir ein!
Und nun mußt du vertrieben sein
  Für all dein Mühn
Und mußt hinaus in nasses Schein
  Und Rauhfrost ziehn!

VII.

Doch, Mäuschen, mehr schon ist zerronnen
In nichts, was Vorsicht klug ersonnen,

Was Mäus' und Menschen fein gesponnen,
  Mißlingt gar oft
Und läßt uns Gram nur statt der Wonnen,
  Die wir gehofft!

VIII.
Doch bist du glücklich gegen mich!
Die Gegenwart nur kümmert dich.
Doch, oh! des Pfads, wenn rückwärts ich
  Zu blicken wage!
Und vor mir, türmt auch dunkel sich,
  Ahn' ich und zage!

Translated by Ferdinand Freiligrath

À une souris

*Dont j'avais détruit le nid avec
ma charrue en Novembre 1785*

[I.]
Petite bête lisse, farouche et craintive
Oh, quelle panique dans ton sein!
Tu n'as pas besoin de te sauver si vite
  Et d'un pas si précipité!
Je me répugnerait de courir après toi
  Avec le cuvoir meurtrier!

[II.]
Je suis vraiment fâché que la domination de l'homme
Ait rompu le pacte social de la nature,
Et qu'elle justifie cette mauvaise opinion
  Qui te fait fuir
Devant moi, ton pauvre compagnon sur la terre,
  Et mortel comme toi!

[III.]
Je sais bien que parfois tu voles!

Mais quoi? Pauvre petite bête, il faut que tu vives!
De temps à autre un épi de blé sur deux douzaines
    Est une faible requête:
Cela portera bonheur au reste
    Et ne me fera jamais faute!

[IV.]

Ta toute petite maisonette aussi, en ruines!
Les vents en éparpillent les misérables murs!
Et rien, à présent, pour en bâtir une nouvelle
    De mousse verte!
Et les vents du froid décembre qui arrivent,
    Après et mordants!

[V.]

Tu voyes les champs nus et dépouillés,
Et l'hiver rigoureux accourir,
Et chaudement ici, à l'abri de son halaine,
    Tu croyais demeurer,
Lorsque, crac! le soc cruel a passé
    À travers ta cellule!

[VI.]

Ce tout petit tas de feuilles et de chaume
T'a coûté bien des grignotements!
Maintenant tu es expulsée, pour fruit de toute ta peine,
    Sans maison ni logis,
Pour supporter les neiges fondues de l'hiver,
    Et les froides gelées blanches.

[VII.]

Mais, petite souris, tu n'es pas la seule
À éprouver que la prévoyance peut être vaine:
Les plans les mieux combinés des souris et des hommes
    Tournent souvent de travers,
Et ne nous laissent que chagrin et peine
    Au lieu de la joie promise.

[VIII.]

Tu es encore heureuse, comparée à moi!
Le present seul te touche;
Mais, hélas! je jette l'œil en arrière
        Sur de lugubres perspectives,
Et ce qui est devant, quoique je ne puisse pas le voir,
        Je le devine et le crains!

Translated by Léon de Wailly

꣠ THE SCOTTISH LANGUAGE is perfect for addressing small children
and animals. German is next because in German diminutives are
familiar and homely and in everyday use.

"Maisonette" is very touching indeed and I am sure it is heart-
breaking to a French person, but American atrocities like "kitchen-
ette" and "luncheonette"—along with "serviette" in England—with
their ducky implications, have almost spoiled all French diminutives
for us. We have done it to ourselves, God forgive us.

In English, diminutives are now so nearly out of fashion that they
have begun sounding self-conscious, except in names like Tommy,
Dickie, and Harry, which have to do with affection and are not neces-
sarily the names of little people. We are inclined to use "little" when
we need it. "Little baby," "little bird," yes; "babykins" and "birdie,"
no—unless we have some particular reason for wanting to be arch, or
unless we are playing golf.

I have given you two translations of this poem into German to
keep from shilly-shallying forever. I can come to no conclusion about
which is better because here and there I think each is better than the
other. I would like to scramble them and make a third poem with
Freiligrath's first stanza and Laun's seventh, which would be better
than either, but, even though such a thing wouldn't be cricket to
print, there's nothing to prevent your doing it in your head.

There is a Beethoven sonata that would (for me) have been the
greatest of them all if only Mozart had written the scherzo.

LORD BYRON

"She walks in beauty"

I.

She walks in beauty—like the night
  Of cloudless climes and starry skies,
And all that's best of dark and bright
  Meet in her aspect and her eyes:
Thus mellow'd to that tender light
  Which heaven to gaudy day denies.
    She walks in beauty—like the night
      Of cloudless climes and starry skies.

II.

One shade the more, one ray the less
  Had half impaired the nameless grace
Which waves in every raven tress,
  Or softly lightens o'er her face—
Where thoughts serenely sweet express
  How pure—how dear their dwellingplace.
    She walks in beauty—like the night
      Of cloudless climes and starry skies.

III.

And on that cheek, and o'er that brow
  So soft—so calm—yet eloquent
The smiles that win—the tints that glow
  But tell of days in goodness spent.
A mind at peace with all below—
  A heart whose love is innocent.
    She walks in beauty—like the night
      Of cloudless climes and starry skies.

"In Schönheit wallt sie hin"

[I.]

In Schönheit wallt sie hin, wie in den lichten
    Und sternenhellen Breiten still die Nacht;
Aus ihren Zügen strahlt, aus ihren Augen,
    Der Helle wie des Dunkels schönste Pracht,
Gedämpft, mit jenem milden Glanz verbunden,
Den Gott versagt den grellen Tagesstunden.

[II.]

Ein Schatten mehr, und wenn ein Strahl nur fehlte,
    So schwände hin der Anmut Zauberlicht,
Das aus den dunkeln Lockenwellen leuchtet
    Und sanft erhellt ihr holdes Angesicht,
Wo die Gedanken klar und heiter thronen
Und kündern, wie's so süß ist, wo sie wohnen.

[III.]

Auf ihrer Wange, auf der edlen Stirne,
    Voll Heiterkeit, beredt, doch lieblich weich,
Zeugt rosig Glüh'n und anmutsvolles Lächeln
    Von Tagen, die an guten Werken reich,
Von einer Seele, welche nichts kann trüben,
Von eines Herzens unschuldsvollem Lieben.

Translated by Herman Behr

L'amie

[I.]

La beauté lui fait cortège, comme la nuit
Des pays fabuleux et des cieux étoilés.
Et tout ce qui ravit, soit ombre, soit clarté,
En sa pose ou ses yeux se voit, sait satisfaire.

Toujours ainsi flattée à la tendre lumière
Que le ciel, en nos jours trop voyants, nous dénie.

[II.]

Une nuance trop, un seul rayon manquant
Dérangerait pour nous cette grâce ineffable
Emprisonnée dans des cheveux noirs ondoyants,
Et d'un charme discret éclairant son visage
Où d'heureuses pensées disent sereinement
La pureté, la douceur d'une âme adorable.

[III.]

Et sur ces joues, et sur ce front
Si délicat, si calme et pourtant éloquent,
Le sourire fascine et le teint concilie,
Révélant des journées de bonté tout emplies;
Une âme en paix avec toutes choses qui sont,
Un cœur dont l'amour est innocent.

*Translated by Félix Rose**

* In 1969 the translator corrected and slightly revised his published translation; these changes have been incorporated here. *Ed.*

"J. NATHAN [Nathan's name was Isaac] is about to publish *Hebrew Melodies*, all of them upward of 1,000 years old and some of them performed by the Ancient Hebrews before the destruction of the Temple." This piece of wildly exaggerated archaeology appeared as an advertisement in the *Gentleman's Magazine* for May, 1813.

Under the title of the poems called *Hebrew Melodies* a note is usually printed stating that Byron wrote them at the suggestion of his friend the Hon. Douglas Kinnaird. This has been proven wrong by a letter discovered more recently. Byron wrote (most of) these poems at the request of an impertinent young upstart called Isaac Nathan, whom he had never met and never heard of. Bowing from the waist in a very greasy letter, Nathan begs His Lordship to prepare some verses for him (Nathan had already been turned down by two

or three other poets, including Thomas Moore) to be sung to "ancient" Hebrew melodies which Nathan had collected and proposed
now to arrange, with piano accompaniment of his own, to pay "a
just tribute of respect to the first poet of the age by having his verses
sung by the greatest vocalist [Isaac Braham, Nathan's partner in the
music publishing business] of the day."

Byron was sufficiently interested in the project to produce twenty-
six poems (a number of which he is suspected of having had on
hand), which, along with the music, were copyrighted April 20, 1814,
by Nathan (smart fellow, Nathan), and the first half of them were
published in January, 1815, by Braham and Nathan in Soho, at 7
Poland Street, Oxford Street, "and to be had at the principal Music
and Book-sellers; price, One Guinea." In May of that year "She walks
in beauty"—called "The Eye of Blue" for some reason or other—was
published separately in the *Gentleman's Magazine*.

Nathan sold the valuable copyrights to his sister Rachel, who sold
them to somebody else, and years after Byron's death, Nathan—of
all people!—started a notorious row with the music seller Novello,
who, in an absent-minded moment, and knowing nothing about these
copyrights, seems to have suggested to Mendelssohn that he saw no
harm in Mendelssohn's writing songs to two of the poems in German.
These two songs of Mendelssohn's, of course, had nothing whatever
to do with Nathan's ancient tunes.

In the first edition the verses are printed on separate pages alter-
nating with pages of music, and the version of "She walks in beauty"
as I have it here, with eight lines to each stanza instead of six, is the
way it appeared.

Wisely enough, on the cover of the published score a change was
made. Contrary to the original advertisement, the "Ancient" Hebrew
Melodies were now a little more accurately described as "Ancient and
Modern," which brought them about a thousand years closer to being
what they were.

Nathan supplied two tunes for "She walks in beauty." "Both," he
says in a footnote to the second, "are sung in different Synagogues
and it is difficult to decide upon their respective claims to originality."
I can see what he means since, for some uncanny reason, most of the

second half of the second tune is most of the first half of the first. Both are made up of four regulation phrases, each of which takes two of Byron's lines. The second phrase is the first repeated and the third, after the customary long pause on the long low note at the end of it, is joined to the fourth by the well-known ascending, flutey cadenza of the period. Both are in three-part time, both are conventional "operatic" arias in the popular Italian style of "I dreamt I dwelt in marble halls," for instance, and neither has anything remotely to do with the destruction of any temple at all. The unknown composer of them both was surely still alive and probably right there at Covent Garden when Mr. Braham (whose name was actually Abraham) sang them there. I have a passing suspicion that Isaac Nathan, who had his early musical training at a synagogue in Cambridge, and played the organ in one all his life, would have taken this opportunity legitimately to include himself. What with "the first poet of the age" and "the greatest vocalist of the day" *and* Covent Garden all converging, why wouldn't he be starting things off with a little something of his own? Besides, if it had been any other composer, wouldn't he have stepped forward at a time like this to reveal himself?

Mrs. Olga Somech Phillips has written a book about all these uninteresting things, called *Isaac Nathan, Friend of Byron*! It was published in London in 1940.

The poem in French fits either tune but, by a still more amusing coincidence, so does the German translation. Both melodies give most of Byron's syllables two or three notes of their own, so that even the German version—which is written in iambic pentameter—can still be sung to either of them perfectly well.

Nathan's music has been forgotten, which is not surprising. The same kind of thing has been written much too often.

The lady who walks in beauty turns out not to be an ancient Hebrew lady at all, as I had always thought, but Byron's stepsister, Augusta.

LEWIS CARROLL

Alice's Adventures in Wonderland

Chapter VI: Pig and Pepper

For a minute or two she stood looking at the house, and wondering what to do next, when suddenly a footman in livery came running out of the wood—(she considered him to be a footman because he was in livery: otherwise, judging by his face only, she would have called him a fish)—and rapped loudly at the door with his knuckles. It was opened by another footman in livery, with a round face and large eyes like a frog; and both footmen, Alice noticed, had powdered hair that curled all over their heads. She felt very curious to know what it was all about, and crept a little way out of the wood to listen.

The Fish-Footman began by producing from under his arm a great letter, nearly as large as himself, and this he handed over to the other saying, in a solemn tone, "For the Duchess. An invitation from the Queen to play croquet." The Frog-Footman repeated, in the same solemn tone, only changing the order of the words a little, "From the Queen. An invitation for the Duchess to play croquet."

Then they both bowed low, and their curls got entangled together.

Alice laughed so much at this, that she had to run back into the wood for fear of their hearing her; and, when she next peeped out, the Fish-Footman was gone, and the other was sitting on the ground near the door, staring stupidly up into the sky.

Alice went timidly up to the door and knocked.

"There's no sort of use in knocking," said the footman, "and that for two reasons. First, because I'm on the same side of the door as you are; secondly, because they're making such a noise inside, no one could possibly hear you." And certainly there was a most extraordinary noise going on within—a constant howl-ing and sneezing, and every now and then a great crash, as if a dish or kettle had been broken to pieces.

"Please, then," said Alice, "how am I to get in?"

"There might be some sense in your knocking," the Footman went on without attending to her, "if we had the door between us. For instance, if you were *inside*, you might knock, and I could let you out, you know." He was looking up into the sky all the time he was speaking, and this Alice thought decidedly uncivil. "But perhaps he can't help it," she said to herself; "his eyes are so *very* nearly at the top of his head. But at any rate he might answer questions. —How am I to get in?" she re-peated, aloud.

"I shall sit here," the Footman remarked, "till to-morrow—"

At this moment the door of the house opened, and a large plate came skimming out, straight at the Footman's head: it just grazed his nose, and broke to pieces against one of the trees be-hind him.

"—or next day, maybe," the Footman continued in the same tone, exactly as if nothing had happened.

"How am I to get in?" asked Alice again in a louder tone.

"*Are* you to get in at all?" said the Footman. "That's the first question, you know."

It was, no doubt: only Alice did not like to be told so. "It's really dreadful," she muttered to herself, "the way all the crea-tures argue. It's enough to drive one crazy!"

The Footman seemed to think this a good opportunity for repeating his remark, with variations. "I shall sit here," he said, "on and off, for days and days."

"But what am *I* to do?" said Alice.

"Anything you like," said the Footman and began whistling.

"Ho, there's no use in talking to him," said Alice desperately: "he's perfectly idiotic!" And she opened the door and went in.

The door led right into a large kitchen, which was full of smoke from one end to the other: the Duchess was sitting on a three-legged stool in the middle, nursing a baby; the cook was leaning over the fire, stirring a large cauldron which seemed to be full of soup.

"There's certainly too much pepper in that soup!" Alice said to herself, as well as she could for sneezing.

There was certainly too much of it in the air. Even the Duchess sneezed occasionally; and the baby was sneezing and howling alternately without a moment's pause. The only things in the kitchen, that did *not* sneeze, were the cook, and a large cat which was sitting on the hearth and grinning from ear to ear.

"Please would you tell me," said Alice a little timidly, for she was not quite sure whether it was good manners for her to speak first, "why your cat grins like that!"

"It's a Cheshire cat," said the Duchess, "and that's why. Pig!"

She said the last word with such sudden violence that Alice quite jumped; but she saw in another moment that it was addressed to the baby, and not to her, so she took courage, and went on again:—

"I didn't know that Cheshire cats always grinned; in fact, I didn't know that cats *could* grin."

"They all can," said the Duchess; "and most of 'em do."

"I don't know of any that do," Alice said very politely, feeling quite pleased to have got into a conversation.

"You don't know much," said the Duchess; "and that's a fact."

Alice did not at all like the tone of this remark, and thought it would be as well to introduce some other subject of conversation. While she was trying to fix on one, the cook took the cauldron of soup off the fire, and at once set to work throwing everything within her reach at the Duchess and the baby—the fire-irons came first; then followed a shower of saucepans, plates, and dishes. The Duchess took no notice of them even when they hit her; and the baby was howling so much already, that it was quite impossible to say whether the blows hurt it or not.

"Oh, *please* mind what you're doing!" cried Alice, jumping up and down in an agony of terror. "Oh, there goes his *precious* nose;" as an unusually large saucepan flew close by it, and very nearly carried it off.

"If everybody minded their own business," the Duchess said
in a hoarse growl, "the world would go round a deal faster than
it does."

"Which would *not* be an advantage," said Alice, who felt very
glad to get an opportunity of showing off a little of her knowledge. "Just think what work it would make with the day and
night! You see the earth takes twenty-four hours to turn round
on its axis—"

"Talking of axes," said the Duchess, "chop off her head."

Alice glanced rather anxiously at the cook, to see if she meant
to take the hint; but the cook was busily engaged in stirring the
soup, and did not seem to be listening, so she ventured to go on
again: "Twenty-four hours, I *think*; or is it twelve? I—"

"Oh, don't bother *me*," said the Duchess; "I never could abide
figures!" And with that she began nursing her child again, singing a sort of lullaby to it as she did so, and giving it a violent
shake at the end of every line:

"Speak roughly to your little boy,
   And beat him when he sneezes;
He only does it to annoy,
   Because he knows it teases."

CHORUS
(In which the cook and the baby joined) :—

"Wow! wow! wow!"

While the Duchess sang the second verse of the song, she
kept tossing the baby violently up and down, and the poor little
thing howled so, that Alice could hardly hear the words:—

"I speak severely to my boy,
   I beat him when he sneezes;
For he can thoroughly enjoy
   The pepper when he pleases!"
CHORUS
"Wow! wow! wow!"

"Here! you may nurse it a bit, if you like!" the Duchess

said to Alice, flinging the baby at her as she spoke. "I must go and get ready to play croquet with the Queen," and she hurried out of the room. The cook threw a frying-pan after her as she went out, but it just missed her.

Alice caught the baby with some difficulty, as it was a queer-shaped little creature, and held out its arms and legs in all directions, "just like a star-fish," thought Alice. The poor little thing was snorting like a steam-engine when she caught it, and kept doubling itself up and straightening itself out again, so that altogether, for the first minute or two, it was as much as she could do to hold it.

As soon as she had made out the proper way of nursing it, (which was to twist it up into a sort of knot, and then keep tight hold of its right ear and left foot, so as to prevent its undoing itself) she carried it out into the open air. "If I don't take this child away with me," thought Alice, "they're sure to kill it in a day or two: wouldn't it be murder to leave it behind?" She said the last words out loud, and the little thing grunted in reply (it had left off sneezing by this time). "Don't grunt," said Alice; "that's not at all a proper way of expressing yourself."

The baby grunted again, and Alice looked very anxiously into its face to see what was the matter with it. There could be no doubt that it had a *very* turn-up nose, much more like a snout than a real nose; also its eyes were getting extremely small for a baby: altogether Alice did not like the look of the thing at all. "But perhaps it was only sobbing," she thought, and looked into its eyes again, to see if there were any tears.

No, there were no tears. "If you're going to turn into a pig, my dear," said Alice, seriously, "I'll have nothing more to do with you. Mind now!" The poor little thing sobbed again (or grunted, it was impossible to say which), and they went on for some while in silence.

Alice was just beginning to think to herself, "Now, what am I to do with this creature when I get it home?" when it grunted again, so violently, that she looked down into its face with some alarm. This time there could be *no* mistake about it: it was neither more nor less than a pig, and she felt that it would be quite absurd for her to carry it any further.

So she set the little creature down, and felt relieved to see it trot quietly away into the wood. "If it had grown up," she said to herself, "it would have made a dreadfully ugly child: but it makes rather a handsome pig, I think." And she began thinking over other children she knew, who might do very well as pigs, and was just saying to herself, "if one only knew the right way to change them—" when she was a little startled by seeing the Cheshire Cat sitting on a bough of a tree a few yards off.

The Cat only grinned when it saw Alice. It looked good-natured, she thought: still it had *very* long claws and a great many teeth, so she felt that it ought to be treated with respect.

"Cheshire Puss," she began, rather timidly, as she did not at all know whether it would like the name: however, it only grinned a little wider. "Come, it's pleased so far," thought Alice, and she went on. "Would you tell me, please, which way I ought to go from here?"

"That depends a good deal on where you want to get to," said the Cat.

"I don't care much where—" said Alice.

"Then it doesn't matter which way you go," said the Cat.

"—so long as I get *somewhere*," Alice added as an explanation.

"Oh, you're sure to do that," said the Cat, "if you only walk long enough."

Alice felt that this could not be denied, so she tried another question. "What sort of people live about here?"

"In *that* direction," the Cat said, waving its right paw round, "lives a Hatter: and in *that* direction," waving the other paw, "lives a March Hare. Visit either you like: they're both mad."

"But I don't want to go among mad people," Alice remarked.

"Oh, you can't help that," said the Cat: "we're all mad here. I'm mad. You're mad."

"How do you know I'm mad?" said Alice.

"You must be," said the Cat, "or you wouldn't have come here."

Alice didn't think that proved it at all; however, she went on. "And how do you know that you're mad?"

"To begin with," said the Cat, "a dog's not mad. You grant that?"

"I suppose so," said Alice.

"Well, then," the Cat went on, "you see a dog growls when it's angry, and wags its tail when it's pleased. Now *I* growl when I'm pleased, and wag my tail when I'm angry. Therefore I'm mad."

"*I* call it purring, not growling," said Alice.

"Call it what you like," said the Cat. "Do you play croquet with the Queen today?"

"I should like it very much," said Alice, "but I haven't been invited yet."

"You'll see me there," said the Cat, and vanished.

Alice was not much surprised at this, she was getting so used to queer things happening. While she was looking at the place where it had been, it suddenly appeared again.

"By-the-bye, what became of the baby?" said the Cat. "I'd nearly forgotten to ask."

"It turned into a pig," Alice quietly said, just as if it had come back in a natural way.

"I thought it would," said the Cat, and vanished again.

Alice waited a little, half expecting to see it again, but it did not appear, and after a minute or two she walked on in the direction in which the March Hare was said to live. "I've seen hatters before," she said to herself; "the March Hare will be much the most interesting, and perhaps, as this is May, it won't be raving mad—at least not so mad as it was in March." As she said this, she looked up, and there was the Cat again, sitting on a branch of a tree.

"Did you say pig, or fig?" said the Cat.

"I said pig," replied Alice; "and I wish you wouldn't keep appearing and vanishing so suddenly: you make one quite giddy."

"All right," said the Cat; and this time it vanished quite

slowly, beginning with the end of the tail, and ending with the grin, which remained some time after the rest of it had gone.

"Well! I've often seen a cat without a grin," thought Alice, "but a grin without a cat! It's the most curious thing I ever saw in all my life."

She had not gone much farther before she came in sight of the house of the March Hare: she thought it must be the right house, because the chimneys were shaped like ears and the roof was thatched with fur. It was so large a house, that she did not like to go nearer till she had nibbled some more of the left-hand bit of mushroom, and raised herself to about two feet high: even then she walked up towards it rather timidly, saying to herself "Suppose it should be raving mad after all! I almost wish I'd gone to see the Hatter instead!"

Alice's Abenteuer im Wunderland

Sechstes Kapitel: Ferkel und Pfeffer

Noch ein bis zwei Augenblicke stand sie und sah das Häuschen an, ohne recht zu wissen, was sie nun thun solle, als plötzlich ein Lackei in Livree vom Walde hergelaufen kam—(sie hielt ihn für einen Lackeien, weil er Livree trug, sonst, nach seinem Gesichte zu urtheilen, würde sie ihn für einen Fisch angesehen haben)—und mit den Knöcheln laut an die Thür klopfte. Sie wurde von einem andern Lackeien in Livree geöffnet, der ein rundes Gesicht und große Augen wie ein Frosch hatte, und beide Lackeien hatten, wie Alice bemerkte, gepuderte Lockenperücken über den ganzen Kopf. Sie war sehr neugierig, was nun geschehen würde, und schlich sich etwas näher, um zuzuhören.

Der Fisch-Lackei fing damit an, einen ungeheuren Brief, beinah so groß wie er selbst, unter dem Arme hervorzuziehen; diesen überreichte er dem andren, in feierlichem Tone sprechend: "Für die Herzogin. Eine Einladung von der Königin, Croquet zu spielen." Der Frosch-Lackei erwiederte in demselben feierlichen Tone, indem er nun die Aufeinanderfolge der Wörter etwas veränderte: "Von der Königin. Eine Einladung für die Herzogin, Croquet zu spielen."

Dann verbeugten sich beide tief, und ihre Locken verwikkelten sich in einander.

Darüber lachte Alice so laut, daß sie in das Gebüsch zurücklaufen mußte, aus Furcht, sie möchten sie hören, und als sie wieder herausguckte, war der Fisch-Lackei fort, und der andere saß auf dem Boden bei der Thür und sah dumm in den Himmel hinauf.

Alice ging furchtsam auf die Thür zu und klopfte.

"Es ist durchaus unnütz, zu klopfen," sagte der Lackei, "und das wegen zweier Gründe. Erstens weil ich an derselben Seite von der Thür bin wie du, zweitens, weil sie drinnen einen solchen Lärm machen, daß man dich unmöglich hören kann." Und wirklich war ein ganz merkwürdiger Lärm drinnen, ein fortwährendes Heulen und Niesen, und von Zeit zu Zeit ein lauter Krachen, als ob eine Schüssel oder ein Kessel zerbrochen wäre.

"Bitte," sagte Alice, "wie soll ich denn hineinkommen?"

"Es wäre etwas Sinn und Verstand darin, anzuklopfen," fuhr der Lackei fort, ohne auf sie zu hören, "wenn wir die Thür zwischen uns hätten. Zum Beispiel, wenn du drinnen wärest, könntest du klopfen; und ich könnte dich herauslassen, nicht wahr?" Er sah die ganze Zeit über, während er sprach, in den Himmel hinauf, was Alice entschieden sehr unhöflich fand. "Aber vielleicht kann er nichts dafür," sagte sie bei sich; "seine Augen sind so hoch oben auf seiner Stirn. Aber jedenfalls könnte er mir antworten.—Wie soll ich denn hineinkommen?" wiederholte sie laut.

"Ich werde hier sitzen," sachte der Lackei, "bis morgen—"

In diesem Augenblick ging die Thür auf, und ein großer Teller kam herausgeflogen, gerade auf den Kopf des Lackeien los; er strich aber über seine Nase hin und brach an einem der dahinterstehenden Bäume in Stücke.

"—oder übermorgen, vielleicht," sprach der Lackei in demselben Ton fort, als ob nichts vorgefallen wäre.

"Wie soll ich denn hineinkommen?" fragte Alice wieder, lauter als vorher.

"Sollst du überhaupt hineinkommen?" sagte der Lackei. "Das ist die erste Frage, nicht wahr?"

Das war es allerdings; nun ließ sich Alice das nicht gern sagen. "Es ist wirklich schrecklich," murmelte sie vor sich hin, "wie naseweis alle diese Geschöpfe sind. Es könnte einen ganz verdreht machen!"

Der Lackei schien für eine gute Gelegenheit anzusehen, seine Bemerkung zu wiederholen, und zwar mit Variationen. "Ich werde hier sitzen," sagte er, "ab und an, Tage und Tage lang."

"Was soll *ich* aber thun?" fragte Alice.

"Was dir gefällig ist," sagte der Lackei, und fing an zu pfeifen.

"Es hilft zu nichts, mit ihm zu reden," sagte Alice außer sich, "er ist vollkommen blödsinnig!" Sie klinkte die Thür auf und ging herein.

Die Thür führte geradeswegs in eine große Küche, welche von einem Ende bis zum andern voller Rauch war; in der Mitte saß auf einem dreibeinigen Schemel die Herzogin, mit einem Wickelkinde auf dem Schoße; die Köchin stand über das Feuer gebückt und rührte in einer großen Kasserole, die voll Suppe zu sein schien.

"In der Suppe ist gewiß zu viel Pfeffer!" sprach Alice für sich, so gut sie vor Niesen konnte.

Es war wenigstens zu viel in der Luft. Sogar die Herzogin nieste hin und wieder; was das Wickelkind anbelangte, so nieste und schrie es abwechselnd ohne die geringste Unterbrechung. Die beiden einzigen Wesen in der Küche, die nicht niesten, waren die Köchin und eine große Katze, die vor dem Herde saß und grinste, so daß die Mundewinkel bis an die Ohren reichten.

"Wollen Sie mir gütigst sagen," fragte Alice etwas furchtsam, denn sie wußte nicht recht, ob es sich für sie schicke zuerst zu sprechen, "warum Ihre Katze so grinst?"

"Es ist eine Grinse-Katze," sagte die Herzogin, "darum! Ferkel!"

Das letzte Wort sagte sie mit solcher Heftigkeit, daß Alice auffuhr; aber den nächsten Augenblick sah sie, daß es dem Wickelkind galt, nicht ihr; sie faßte also Muth und redete weiter:—

"Ich wußte nicht, daß Katzen manchmal grinsen; ja ich wußte nicht, daß Katzen überhaupt grinsen *können.*"

"Sie können es alle," sagte die Herzogin, "und die meisten thun es."

"Ich kenne keine, die es thut," sagte Alice sehr höflich, da sie ganz froh war, eine Unterhaltung angeknüpft zu haben.

"Du kennst noch nicht viel," sagte die Herzogin, "und das ist die Wahrheit."

Alice gefiel diese Bemerkung gar nicht, und sie dachte daran, welchen andern Gegenstand der Unterhaltung sie einführen könnte, während sie sich auf etwas Passendes besann, nahm die Köchin die Kasserole mit Suppe vom Feuer und fing sogleich an, alles was sie erreichen konnte nach der Herzogin und dem Kinde zu werfen—die Feuerzange kam zuerst, dann folgte ein Hagel von Pfannen, Tellern und Schüsseln. Die Herzogin beachtete sie gar nicht, auch wenn sie sie trafen; und das Kind heulte schon so laut, daß es unmöglich war zu wissen, ob die Stöße ihm weh thaten oder nicht.

"Oh, bitte, nehmen Sie sich in Acht, was Sie thun!" rief Alice, die in wahrer Herzensangst hin und her sprang. "Oh, seine liebe kleine Nase!" als eine besonders große Pfanne dicht daran vorbeifuhr und sie beinah abstieß.

"Wenn Jeder nun vor seiner Thür fegen wollte," brummte die Herzogin mit heiserer Stimme, "würde die Welt sich bedeutend schneller drehen, als jetzt."

"Was kein Vortheil wäre," sprach Alice, die sich über die Gelegenheit freute, ihre Kenntnisse zu zeigen. "Denken Sie nun, wie es Tag und Nacht in Unordnung bringen würde! Die Erde braucht doch jetzt vier und zwanzig Stunden, sich in ihre Achse zu drehen—"

"Was, du redest von Axt?" fragte die Herzogin. "Hau' ihr den Kopf ab!"

Alice sah sich sehr erschroken nach der Köchin um, ob sie den Wink verstehen würde; aber die Köchin rührte die Suppe unverwandt und schien nicht zuzuhören, daher fuhr sie fort: "Vier und zwanzig Stunden, glaube ich; oder sind es zwölf? Ich—"

"Ach, laß mich in Frieden," sagte die Herzogin, "ich habe Zahlen nie ausstehen können!" Und damit fing sie an, ihr Kind zu warten und eine Art Wiegenlied dazu zu singen, wovon jede Reihe mit einem derben Puffe für das Kind endigte:—

"Schilt deinen kleinen Jungen aus,
Und schlag' ihn wenn er niest;
Er macht es gar so bunt und kraus,
Nur weil es uns verdrießt."

CHOR
(*in welchen die Köchin und das Wickelkind einfielen*)
"Wau! wau! wau"

Während die Herzogin den zweiten Vers des Liedes sang, schaukelte sie das Kind so heftig auf und nieder, und das arme kleine Ding schrie so, daß Alice kaum die Worte verstehen konnte:—

"Ich schelte meinen kleinen Wicht,
Und schlag' ihn, wenn er niest;
Ich weiß, wie gern er Pfeffer riecht,
Wenn's ihm gefällig ist."

CHOR
"Wau! wau! wau!"

"Hier! du kannst ihn ein Weilchen warten, wenn du willst!" sagte die Herzogin zu Alice, indem sie ihr das Kind zuwarf. "Ich muß mich zurecht machen, um mit der Königin Croquet zu

spielen," damit rannte sie aus dem Zimmer. Die Köchin warf
ihr eine Bratpfanne nach; aber sie verfehlte sie noch eben.

Alice hatte das Kind mit Mühe und Noth aufgefangen, da es
ein kleines unförmliches Wesen war, das seine Arme und Bein-
chen nach allen Seiten ausstreckte, "gerade wie ein Seestern,"
dachte Alice. Das arme kleine Ding ströhnte wie eine Loco-
motive, als sie es fing, und zog sich zusammen und streckte sich
wieder aus, so daß sie es die ersten Paar Minuten nur eben
halten konnte.

Sobald sie aber die rechte Art entdeckt hatte, wie man es
tragen mußte (die darin bestand, es zu einer Art Knoten zu
drehen, und es dann fest beim rechten Ohr und linken Fuß zu
fassen, damit es sich nicht wieder aufwickeln konnte), brachte
sie es ins Freie. "Wenn ich dies Kind nicht mit mir nehme,"
dachte Alice, "so werden sie es in wenigen Tagen umgebracht
haben; wäre es nicht Mord, es da zu lassen?" Sie sprach die
letzten Worte laut, und das kleine Geschöpf grunzte zur Ant-
wort (es hatte mittlerweile aufgehört zu niesen). "Grunze
nicht," sagte Alice; "es paßt sich gar nicht für dich, dich so aus-
zudrücken."

Der Junge grunzte wieder, so daß Alice ihm ganz ängstlich
in's Gesicht sah, was ihm eigentlich fehle. Er hatte ohne Zweifel
eine *sehr* hervorstehende Nase, eher eine Schnauze als eine
wirkliche Nase; auch seine Augen wurden entsetzlich klein
für einen kleinen Jungen: Alles zusammen genommen, gefiel
Alice das Aussehen des Kindes gar nicht. "Aber vielleicht hat
es nur geweint," dachte sie und sah ihm wieder in die Augen,
ob Thränen da seien.

Nein, es waren keine Thränen da. "Wenn du ein kleines Ferkel wirst, höre mal," sagte Alice sehr ernst, "so will ich nichts
mehr mit dir zu schaffen haben, das merke dir!" Das arme
kleine Ding schluchzte (oder grunzte, es war unmöglich, es zu
unterscheiden), und dann gingen sie eine Weile stillschweigend
weiter.

Alice fing eben an, sich zu überlegen: "Nun, was soll ich mit
diesem Geschöpf anfangen, wenn ich es mit nach Hause

bringe?" als es wieder grunzte, so laut, daß Alice erschrocken nach ihm hinsah. Diesmal konnte sie sich nicht mehr irren: es war nichts mehr weniger als ein Ferkel, und sie sah, daß es höchst lächerlich für sie wäre, es noch weiter zu tragen. Sie setzte also das kleine Ding hin und war ganz froh, als sie es ruhig in den Wald traben sah. "Das wäre in einigen Jahren ein furchtbar häßliches Kind geworden; aber als Ferkel macht es sich recht nett, finde ich." Und so dachte sie alle Kinder durch, die sie kannte, die gute kleine Ferkel abgeben würden, und sagte gerade für sich: "wenn man nur die rechte Mittel wüßte, sie zu verwandeln—" als sie einen Schreck bekam; die Grinse-Katze saß nämlich wenige Fuß von ihr auf einem Baumzweige.

Die Katze grinste nur, als sie Alice sah. "Sie sieht gutmütig aus," dachte diese; "aber doch hatte sie *sehr* lange Krallen und eine Menge Zähne." Alice fühtle wohl, daß sie sie rücksichtvoll behandeln müsse.

"Grinse-Mies," fing sie etwas ängstlich an, da sie nicht wußte, ob ihr den Name gefallen würde; jedoch grinste sie noch etwas breiter. "Schön, so weit gefällt es ihr," dachte Alice und sprach weiter: "willst du mir wohl sagen, wenn ich bitten darf, welchen Weg ich hier nehmen muß?"

"Das hängt zum guten Theil davon ab, wohin du gehen willst," sagte die Katze.

"Es kommt mir nicht darauf an, wohin—" sagte Alice.

"Dann kommt es auch nicht darauf an, welchen Weg du nimmst," sagte die Katze.

"—wenn ich nur *irgendwo* hinkomme," fügte Alice als Erklärung hinzu.

"O, das wirst du ganz gewiß," sagte die Katze, "wenn du nur lange genug gehest."

Alice sah, daß sie nichts dagegen einwenden konnte; sie versuchte daher eine andere Frage. "Was für Art Leute wohnen hier in der Nähe?"

"In *der* Richtung," sagte die Katze, die rechte Pfote schwenkend, "wohnt ein Hutmacher, und in jener Richtung," die andere Pfote schwenkend, "wohnt ein Faselhase. Besuche welchen du willst: sie sind beide toll."

"Aber ich mag nicht zu tollen Leuten gehen," bemerkte Alice.

"Oh, das kannst du nicht ändern," sagte die Katze: "wir sind alle toll hier. Ich bin toll. Du bist toll."

"Woher weißt du, dass ich toll bin?" fragte Alice.

"Du mußt es sein," sagte die Katze, "sonst wärest du nicht hergekommen."

Alice fand durchaus nicht, daß das ein Beweis sei; sie fragte jedoch weiter: "Und woher weißt du, daß du toll bist?"

"Zu allererst," sagte die Katze, "ein Hund ist nicht toll. Das gibst du zu?"

"Zugestanden!" sagte Alice.

"Nun, gut," fuhr die Katze fort, "nicht wahr ein Hund knurrt, wenn er böse ist, und wedelt mit dem Schwanze, wenn er sich freut. Ich hingegen knurre, wenn ich mich freue, und wedle mit dem Schwanze, wenn ich ärgerlich bin. Daher bin ich toll."

"Ich nenne es spinnen, nicht knurren," sagte Alice.

"Nenne es, wie du willst," sagte die Katze. "Spielst du heute Croquet mit der Königin?"

"Ich möchte sehr gern," sagte Alice, "aber ich bin noch nicht eingeladen worden."

"Du wirst mich dort sehen," sagte die Katze und verschwand.

Alice wunderte sich nicht sehr darüber; sie war so daran gewöhnt, daß sonderbare Dinge geschahen. Während sie noch nach der Stelle hinsah, wo die Katze gesessen hatte, erschien sie plötzlich wieder.

"Übrigens, was ist aus dem Jungen geworden?" sagte die Katze. "Ich hätte beinah vergessen zu fragen."

"Er ist ein Ferkel geworden," antwortete Alice sehr ruhig, gerade wie wenn die Katze auf gewöhnliche Weise zurückgekommen wäre.

"Das dachte ich wohl," sagte die Katze und verschwand wieder.

Alice wartete noch etwas, halb und halb erwartend, sie wieder erscheinen zu sehen; aber sie kam nicht, und ein Paar Minuten nachher ging sie in der Richtung fort, wo der Faselhase wohnen sollte. "Hutmacher habe ich schon gesehen," sprach sie zu sich, "der Faselhase wird viel interessanter sein." Wie sie so sprach, blickte sie auf, und da saß die Katze wieder auf einem Baumzweige. "Sagtest du Ferkel oder Fächer?" fragte sie. "Ich sagte Ferkel," antwortete Alice, "und es wäre mir sehr lieb, wenn du nicht immer so schnell erscheinen und verschwinden wolltest: du machst einen ganz schwindlig."

"Schon gut," sagte die Katze, und diesmal verschwand sie ganz langsam, wobei sie mit der Schwanzspitze anfing und mit dem Grinsen aufhörte, das noch einige Zeit sichtbar blieb, nachdem das Übrige verschwunden war.

"Oho, ich habe oft eine Katze ohne Grinsen gesehen," dachte Alice, "aber ein Grinsen ohne Katze! so etwas Merkwürdiges habe ich in meinem Leben noch nicht gesehen!"

Sie brauchte nicht weit zu gehen, so erblickte sie das Haus des Faselhasen; sie dachte, es müsse das rechte Haus sein, weil die Schornsteine wie Ohren geformt waren, und das Dach war mit Pelz gedeckt. Es war ein so großes Haus, daß, ehe sie sich näher heran wagte, sie ein wenig von dem Stück Pilz in ihrer linken Hand abknabberte, und sich bis auf zwei Fuß hoch brachte: trotzdem näherte sie sich etwas furchtsam, für sich sprechend: "Wenn er nur nicht ganz rasend ist! Wäre ich doch lieber zu dem Hutmacher gegangen!"

Translated by Antonie Zimmermann

Aventures d'Alice au pays des merveilles

Chapitre VI: Porc et poivre

Alice resta une ou deux minutes à regarder à la porte; elle se demandait ce qu'il fallait faire, quand tout à coup un laquais en livrée sortit du bois en courant. (Elle le prit pour un laquais à cause de sa livrée; sans cela, à n'en juger que par la figure, elle

l'aurait pris pour un poisson.) Il frappa fortement avec son doigt
à la porte. Elle fut ouverte par un autre laquais en livrée qui
avait la face toute ronde et de gros yeux comme une grenouille.
Alice remarqua que les deux laquais avaient les cheveux
poudrés et tout frisés. Elle se sentit piquée de curiosité, et,
voulant savoir ce que tout cela signifiait, elle se glissa un peu en
dehors du bois afin d'écouter.

Le Laquais-Poisson prit de dessous son bras une lettre
énorme, presque aussi grande que lui, et la présenta au Laquais-
Grenouille en disant d'un ton solennel: "Pour Madame la
Duchesse, une invitation de la Reine à une partie de croquet."
Le Laquais-Grenouille répéta sur le même ton solennel, en
changeant un peu l'ordre des mots: "De la part de la Reine une
invitation pour Madame la Duchesse à une partie de croquet";
puis tous deux se firent un profond salut et les boucle de leurs
chevelures s'entremêlèrent.

Cela fit tellement rire Alice qu'elle eut à rentrer bien vite dans
le bois de peur d'être entendu; et quand elle avança la tête
pour regarder de nouveau, le Laquais-Poisson était parti, et
l'autre était assis par terre près de la route, regardant niaisement
en l'air.

Alice s'approcha timidement de la porte et frappa.

"Cela ne sert à rien du tout de frapper," dit le Laquais, "et
cela pour deux raisons: premièrement, parce que je suis du
même côté de la porte que vous; deuxièmement, parce qu'on
fait là-dedans un tel bruit que personne ne peut vous entendre."
En effet, il se faisait dans l'intérieur un bruit extraordinaire, des
hurlements et des éternuements continuels, et de temps à autre
un grand fracas comme si on brisait de la vaisselle.

"Eh bien! comment puis-je entrer, s'il vous plaît?" demanda
Alice.

"Il y aurait quelque bon sens à frapper à cette porte," continua le Laquais sans l'écouter, "si nous avions la porte entre
nous deux. Par example, si vous étiez à l'intérieur vous pourriez
frapper et je pourrais vous laisser sortir." Il regardait en l'air
tout le temps qu'il parlait, et Alice trouvait cela très impoli.

"Mais peut-être ne peut-il pas s'en empêcher," dit-elle; "il a les yeux presque sur sommet de la tête. Dans tout les cas il pourrait bien répondre à mes questions. —Comment faire pour entrer?" répéta-t-elle tout haut.

"Je vais rester assis ici," dit le Laquais, "jusqu'à demain—"

Au même instant la porte de la maison s'ouvrit, et une grande assiette vola tout droit dans la direction de la tête du Laquais; elle lui effleura le nez, et alla se briser contre un arbre derrière lui.

"—ou le jour suivant peut-être," continua le Laquais sur le même ton, tout comme si rien n'était arrivé.

"Comment faire pour entrer?" redemanda Alice en élevant la voix.

"Mais devriez-vous entrer?" dit le Laquais. "C'est ce qu'il faut se demander, n'est-ce pas?"

Bien certainement, mais Alice trouva mauvais qu'on le lui dît. "C'est vraiment terrible," murmura-t-elle, "de voir la manière dont ces gens-là discutent, il y a de quoi rendre fou."

Le Laquais trouva l'occasion bonne pour répéter son observation avec des variantes. "Je resterai assis ici," dit-il, "l'un dans l'autre, pendant des jours et des jours!"

"Mais que faut-il que je fasse?" dit Alice.

"Tout ce que vous voudrez," dit le Laquais; et il se mit à siffler.

"Oh! ce n'est pas la peine de lui parler," dit Alice désespérée; "c'est un parfait idiot." Puis elle ouvrit la porte et entra.

La porte donnait sur une grande cuisine qui était pleine de fumée d'un bout à l'autre. La Duchesse était assise sur un tabouret à trois pieds, au milieu de la cuisine, et dorlotait un bébé; la cuisinière, penchée sur le feu, brassait quelque chose dans un grand chaudron qui paraissait rempli de soupe.

"Bien sûr, il y a trop de poivre dans la soupe," se dit Alice, tout empêchée par les éternuements.

Il y en avait certainement trop dans l'air. La Duchesse elle-même éternuait de temps en temps, et quant au bébé il éternuait et hurlait alternativement sans aucune interruption. Les deux seules créatures qui n'éternuassent pas, étaient la cuisinière et un gros chat assis sur l'âtre et dont la bouche grimaçante était fendue d'une oreille à l'autre.

"Pourriez-vous m'apprendre," dit Alice un peu timidement, car elle ne savait pas s'il était bien convenable qu'elle parlât la première, "pourquoi votre chat grimaçe ainsi?"

"C'est un Grimaçon," dit la Duchesse; "voilà pourquoi. —Porc!"

Elle prononça ce dernier mot si fort et si subitement qu'Alice en frémit. Mais elle comprit bientôt que cela s'adressait au bébé et non pas à elle; elle reprit donc courage et continua:

"J'ignorais qu'il y eût des chats de cette espèce. Au fait j'ignorais qu'un chat pût grimacer."

"Ils le peuvent tous," dit la Duchesse; "et la plupart le font."

"Je n'en connais pas un qui grimace," dit Alice poliment, bien contente d'être entrée en conversation.

"La fait est que vous ne savez pas grand'chose," dit la Duchesse.

Le ton sur lequel faite faire cette observation ne plut pas du tout à Alice, et elle pensa qu'il serait bon de changer la conversation. Tandis qu'elle cherchait un autre sujet, la cuisinière retira de dessus le feu le chaudron plein de soupe, et se mit aussitôt à jeter tout ce qui lui tomba sous la main à la Duchesse et au bébé—la pelle et les pincettes d'abord, à leur suite vint une pluie de casseroles, d'assiettes et de plats. La Duchesse n'y faisait pas la moindre attention, même quand elle en était atteinte, et l'enfant hurlait déjà si fort auparavant qu'il était impossible de savoir si les coups lui faisaient mal ou non.

"Oh! je vous en prie, prenez garde à ce que vous faites," criait Alice, sautant çà et là et en proie à la terreur. "Oh! son cher petit nez!" Une casserole d'une grandeur peu ordinaire venait de voler tout près du bébé, et avait failli lui emporter le nez.

"Si chacun s'occupait de ses affaires," dit la Duchesse avec un grognement rauque, "le mond n'en irait que mieux."

"Ce qui ne serait guère avantageux," dit Alice, enchantée

qu'il se présentât une occasion de montrer un peu de son savoir.
"Songez à ce que deviendraient le jour et la nuit; vous voyez
bien, la terre met vingt-quatre heures à faire sa révolution."

"Ah! vous parlez de faire des révolutions!" dit la Duchesse.
"Qu'on lui coupe la tête!"

Alice jeta un regard inquiet sur la cuisinère pour voir si elle
allait obéir; mais la cuisinière était tout occupée à brasser la
soupe et paraissait ne pas écouter. Alice continua donc: "Vingt-
quatre heures, je crois, ou bien douze? Je pense—"

"Oh! laissez-moi la paix," dit la Duchesse, "je n'ai jamais pu
souffrir les chiffres." Et là-dessus elle recommença à dorloter
son enfant, lui chantant une espèce de chanson pour l'endormir
et lui donnant une forte secousse au bout de chaque vers.

> "Grondez-moi ce vilain garçon!
> Battez-le quand il éternue;
> À vous traquiner, sans façon
> Le méchant enfant s'évertue."

R E F R A I N
(que reprirent en chœur la cuisinière et le bébé).
"Brou, Brou, Brou!" (*bis.*)

En chantant le second couplet de la chanson la Duchesse
faisait sauter le bébé et le secouait violemment, si bien que le
pauvre petit être hurlait au point qu'Alice put à peine entendre
ces mots:

> "Oui, oui, je m'en vrais le gronder,
> Et le battre, s'il éternue;
> Car bientôt à savoir poivrer,
> Je veux que l'enfant s'habitue."

R E F R A I N
"Brou, Brou, Brou!" (*bis.*)

"Tenez, vous pouvrez le dorloter si vous voulez!" dit la
Duchesse à Alice: et à ces mots elle lui jeta la bébé. "Il faut que
j'aille m'apprêter pour aller jouer au croquet avec la Reine."
Et elle se précipita hors de la chambre. La cuisinière lui lança

une poêle comme elle s'en allait, mais elle la manqua tout juste.

Alice eut de la peine à attraper le bébé. C'était un petit être d'une forme étrange qui tenait ses bras et ses jambes étendus dans toutes les directions; "Tout comme une étoile de mer," pensait Alice. La pauvre petite créature ronflait comme une machine à vapeur lorsqu'elle l'attrapa, et ne cessait de se plier en deux, puis de s'étendre tout droit, de sorte qu'avec tout cela, pendant les premiers instants, c'est tout ce qu'elle pouvait faire que de le tenir.

Sitôt qu'elle eut trouvé le bon moyen de le bercer, (qui était d'en faire une espèce de nœud, et puis de le tenir fermement par l'oreille droite et le pied gauche afin de l'empêcher de se denouer,) elle la porta dehors en plein air. "Si je n'emporte pas cet enfant avec moi," pensa Alice, "ils le tueront bien sûr un de ces jours. Ne serait-ce pas un meurtre de l'abandonner?" Elle dit ces derniers mots à haute voix, et la petite créature répondit en grognant (elle avait cessé d'éternuer alors). "Ne grogne pas ainsi," dit Alice; "ce n'est pas là du tout une bonne manière de s'exprimer."

Le bébé grogna de nouveau. Alice le regarda au visage avec inquiétude pour voir ce qu'il avait. Sans contredit son nez était très retroussé, et ressemblait bien plutôt à un groin qu'à un vrai nez. Ses yeux aussi devenaient très petits pour un bébé. Enfin Alice ne trouva pas du tout de son goût l'aspect de ce petit être. "Mais peut-être sanglotait-il tout simplement," pensa-t-elle, et elle regarda de nouveau les yeux du bébé pour voir s'il n'y avait pas de larmes. "Si tu vas te changer en porc," dit Alice très sèrieusement, "je ne veux plus rien avoir à faire avec toi. Fais-y bien attention!"

La pauvre petite créature sanglota de nouveau, ou grogna (il était impossible de savoir lequel des deux), et ils continuèrent leur chemin un instant en silence.

Alice commençait à dire en elle-même, "Mais, que faire de cette créature quand je l'aurai portée à la maison?" lorsqu'il grogna de nouveau si fort qu'elle regarda sa figure avec quelque inquiétude. Cette fois il n'y avait pas à s'y tromper, c'était un porc, ni plus ni moins, et elle comprit qu'il serait ridicule de le porter plus loin.

Elle déposa donc par terre le petit animal, et se sentit toute soulagée de le voir trotter tranquillement vers le bois. "S'il avait grandi," se dit-elle, "il serait devenu un bien vilain enfant; tandis qu'il fait un assez joli petit porc, il me semble." Alors elle se mit à penser à d'autres enfants qu'elle connaissait et qui feraient d'assez jolis porcs, si seulement on savait la manière de s'y prendre pour les métamorphoser. Elle était en train de faire ces réflexions, lorsqu'elle tressaillit en voyant tout à coup le Chat assis à quelques pas de là sur la branche d'un arbre.

Le Chat grimaça en apercevant Alice. Elle trouva qu'il avait l'air bon enfant, et cependant il avait de très longues griffes et une grande rangée de dents; aussi comprit-elle qu'il fallait le traiter avec respect.

"Grimaçon!" commença-t-elle un peu timidement, ne sachant pas du tout si cette familiarité lui serait agréable; toutefois il ne fit qu'allonger sa grimace.

"Allons, il est content jusqu'à présent," pensa Alice, et elle continua: "Dites-moi, je vous prie, de quel côté faut-il me diriger?"

"Cela dépend beaucoup de l'endroit où vous voulez aller," dit le Chat.

"Cela m'est assez indifférent," dit Alice.

"Alors peu importe de quel côté vous irez," dit le Chat.

"Pourvu que j'arrive *quelque part*," ajouta Alice en explication.

"Cela ne peut manquer, pourvu que vous marchiez assez longtemps."

Alice comprit que cela était incontestable; elle essaya donc d'une autre question: "Quels sont les gens qui demeurent par ici?"

"De ce côté-ci," dit le Chat, décrivant un cercle avec sa patte droite, "demeure un chapelier; de ce côté-là," faisant de même avec sa patte gauche, "demeure un lièvre. Allez voir celui que vous voudrez, tout deux sont fous."

"Mais je ne veux pas fréquenter des fous," fit observer Alice.

"Vous ne pouvez pas vous en défendre, tout le monde est fou ici. Je suis fou, vous êtes folle."

"Comment savez-vous que je suis folle?" dit Alice.

"Vous devez l'être," dit le Chat, "sans cela vous ne seriez pas venue ici."

Alice pensa que cela ne prouvait rien. Toute-fois elle continua: "Et comment savez-vous que vous êtes fou?"

"D'abord," dit le Chat, "un chien n'est pas fou; vous convenez de cela."

"Je le suppose," dit Alice.

"Eh bien!" continua le Chat, "un chien grogne quand il se fâche, et remue la queue lorsqu'il est content. Or, moi, je grogne quand je suis content, et je remue la queue quand je me fâche. Donc je suis fou."

"J'appelle cela faire le rouet, et non pas grogner," dit Alice.

"Appelez cela comme vous voudrez," dit le Chat. "Jouez-vous au croquet avec la Reine aujourd'hui?"

"Cela me ferait grand plaisir," dit Alice, "mais je n'ai pas été invitée."

"Vous m'y verrez," dit le Chat; et il disparut.

Alice ne fut pas très-étonnée, tant elle commençait à s'habituer aux événements extraordinaires. Tandis qu'elle regardait encore l'endroit que le Chat venait de quitter, il reparut tout á coup.

"À propos, qu'est devenu le bébé? J'allais oublier de le demander."

"Il a été changé en porc," dit tranquillement Alice, comme si le Chat était revenu d'une manière naturelle.

"Je m'en doutais," dit le Chat; et il disparut de nouveau.

Alice attendit quelques instants, espérent presque le revoir, mais il ne reparut pas; et une ou deux minutes après, elle continua son chemin dans la direction où on lui avait dit que demeurait le Lièvre. "J'ai déjà vue des chapeliers." À ces mots elle leva les yeux, et voilà que le Chat était encore là assis sur une branche d'arbre.

"M-avez-vous dit porc, ou porte?" demanda le Chat.

"J'ai dit porc," répéta Alice. "Ne vous amusez donc pas à paraître et à disparaître si subitement, vous faites tourner la tête aux gens."

"C'est bon," dit le Chat, et cette fois il s'évanouit tout douce-ment à commencer par le bout de la queue, et finissant par sa grimace qui demeura quelque temps après que le reste fut dis-paru.

"Certes," pensa Alice, "j'ai souvent vu un chat sans grimace, mais une grimace sans chat, je n'ai jamais de ma vie rien vu de si drôle."

Elle ne fit pas beaucoup de chemin avant d'arriver devant la maison du Lièvre. Elle pensa que ce devait bien être là la maison, car les cheminées étaient en forme d'oreilles et le toit était couvert de fourrure. La maison était si grande qu'elle n'osa s'approcher avant d'avoir grignoté encore un peu du mor-ceau de champignon qu'elle avait dans la main gauche, et d'avoir atteint la taille de deux pieds environ; et même alors elle avança timidement en se disant: "Si après tout il était fou furieux! Je voudrais presque avoir été faire visite au Chapelier plutôt que d'être venue ici."

Translated by Henri Bué

AT ADSDENE IN WINTER we used to have tea in the billiard room, the children at one end at their own little table in front of the fire, the grownups at the other, at the grownups' table with a silver urn and blue and white Worcester cups. After tea—which was bread and butter and a sultana cake at the children's end—when the table was cleared away, the little girls used to move to the fire bench. At Adsdene it was cold in winter—cold as anything. The children's grandmother and I, because I preferred their grandmother's racy, old-fashioned way of reading *Alice* aloud to anything the grownups might be saying, would change into armchairs at either side.

It was nearly Christmas and his uncle had just given David a tricycle. After tea David liked to sit on it. If the reading was beyond
him he could always get away from it without disturbing anybody
by riding once or twice around the billiard table. A few days before—
probably five—the children's grandmother had begun reading a chapter a day of *Alice* to them, and David, who was really too little for
such sophisticated, heady stuff, had to ride his tricycle most of the
time because he was certainly not allowed to interrupt.

Their grandmother opened the book to Chapter VI. She had something marking the place from the day before that I think was a bay
leaf.

" 'Pig and Pepper,' " she said suddenly.

"What's *that* going to be?" said Pamela, trying to curl her legs up
under her.

"It is the name of the next chapter. And do put your feet down,
dear, or you will certainly fall into the fire. And Patricia, dear, please,
please to stop fiddling. Yesterday—do you remember?—we read the
'Advice from a Caterpillar' chapter."

The children's grandmother read it wonderfully in different voices,
so that when she was Alice she was demure and very polite, and when
she was the Duchess she bellowed among the flying plates. When
the Fish-Footman spoke she burbled under water, but when the
Frog-Footman spoke she outdid herself. She had him sounding almost like a very old Negro, and when an English lady sounds almost
like a very old Negro, she is speaking in exactly the voice of the Frog-
Footman. He was far and away her greatest rôle and she had the little
girls shouting with laughter. You were not forbidden to laugh during the reading, and David rode round and round laughing too.

At the end of the chapter, with Alice on her way to the March
Hare's house, David and his cousins said good night to everyone;
the little girls flung themselves at their grandmother and thanked her
for reading to them. At the door they curtsied to her, and David and
they were taken away.

After a while the grownups began moving upstairs to change for
dinner. They were all talking at once as they did every afternoon,

disagreeing about all the things there were in England that year to disagree about. The children's grandmother and I were left alone.

She sat there cheating a little, chuckling to herself, reading ahead for tomorrow. Then, putting back the bay leaf to mark the place, she closed the book.

"Have you ever read *Alice* in German?" she said. She took a pack of cigarettes and a long ivory holder out of a pocket in her petticoat.

"No," I said, lighting her cigarette for her. "Heavens, no!—have you?"

"Yes, yes, of course. I have had it read to me again and again out of the beautiful copy Lewis Carroll presented to my mother's sister Beatrice when she was a child. We have it somewhere. I must try to find it for you."

"How can it be possible to translate *Alice* into German? I don't see how the jokes made of English plays on English words could ever be made to work in German."

"It has been done very cleverly—very, very cleverly." We stopped on the way upstairs. "*Alice* is delicious in German!"

"How, for instance, do you make a joke like the 'speaking-of-axes' joke in German?"

"Wait," she said on the landing, and closed her eyes. "Wait. I think I can remember it for you. " 'Was, du redest von Axt?' fragte die Herzogin. 'Hau' ihr den Kopf ab!' " Do you see how well it goes? Perhaps by dinner time I shall be able to remember 'The Lobster Quadrille.' "

I used to be put next to this remarkable old lady whenever dinner was small enough or inconsequential enough for her to be given me. That night, in the midst of three conversations about the new polo rules, the morning's new litter of Sealyham puppies, and the number of additional portholes in the new destroyers, which she was carrying on simultaneously with three different people, she laid her hand on my arm and began softly to say:

> Zu der Schnecke sprach ein Weißfisch:
> "Kannst du denn nicht schneller gehn?
> Siehst du denn nicht die Schildkröten
> und die Hummer alle stehn?

Hinter uns da kommt ein Meerschwein,
und es tritt mir auf den Schwanz;
Und sie warten auf dem Strande,
daß wir kommen zu dem Tanz.
Willst du denn nicht, willst du denn nicht,
willst du kommen zu dem Tanz?
Willst du denn nicht, willst du denn nicht,
willst du kommen zu dem Tanz?"

"Oh, yes," she said. "I must find it for you."

These were the Christmas holidays of 1935. The following winter the abdication came and, in the spring, the coronation came, and then, after a while, came the War. Naturally I was back in America and we all forgot about the German *Alice*. Even I forgot until many years later. The remarkable old lady has died. The little girls are grown and married now. Even David is married.

On April 6, 1869, Lewis Carroll wrote in his diary: "On the 31st March I heard from Lady A. Stanley, that the Queen will allow Princess Beatrice to accept a German *Alice*; which accordingly is being bound for her."

So this was the beautiful book we forgot to find!

I can discover no trace of Fräulein Antonie Zimmermann, the sympathetic German translator of *Alice*, except in the diaries,* where she appears only twice, very briefly. The first time on April 13, 1867: "Heard from Aunt Caroline of a Miss Zimmermann, a teacher of German who would like to translate *Alice*: suggested that she should name terms and translate as specimens pp. 36 and 183." Her second appearance, almost a year and a half later, is on Sept. 4, 1868. Apparently her completed translation was being submitted on that day. Carroll writes: "Had two hours with Miss Zimmermann, looking over German version of *Alice*." This is all we hear of Fräulein Zimmermann, I regret to say.

M. Henri Bué, the French translator, is less obscure, although he never appears in the diaries at all.

Henri Bué, *B. ès L., Officer d' Académie*, who had been the French

* Roger Lancelyn Green, *The Diaries of Lewis Carroll* (New York: Oxford University Press, 1954).

Examiner in the University of London, among other things, is, in
1897, Principal French Master at Christ's Hospital, London, and pub-
lishes in that year his students' textbooks of Racine's *Phèdre*, "with
argument of each act and grammatical and explanatory notes." In
1912, after his retirement, he published a similarly annotated text of
Banville's *Gringoire*.

Of the whole of *Alice* I have chosen "Pig and Pepper" because in
it M. Bué reaches the great moment in his whole translation. It occurs
in this passage:

Carroll:

> "If everybody minded their own business," the Duchess said in a
> hoarse growl, "the world would go round a deal faster than it does."
>
> "Which would not be an advantage," said Alice . . . "Just think
> what work it would make with the day and night! You see the earth
> takes twenty-four hours to turn round on its axis—"
>
> "Talking of axes," said the Duchess, "chop off her head."

Bué:

> "Si chacun s'occupait de ses affaires," dit la Duchesse avec un
> grognement rauque, "le mond n'en irait que mieux."
>
> "Ce qui ne serait guère avantageux," dit Alice . . . "Songez à ce
> que deviendraient le jour et la nuit; vous voyez bien, la terre met
> vingt-quatre heures à faire sa révolution."
>
> "Ah! vous parlez de faire des révolutions!" dit la Duchesse. "Qu'on
> lui coupe la tête!"

Here Bué—with a stroke of wizardry and judgment which, in this
instance, is not translation by *word*, but translation by *change of word*
—has instantaneously transformed a witty English idea *in its entirety*
into a perfectly parallel, equally witty French idea. And when "the
Duchess" changes into "la Duchesse," the axe, *by association*, becomes a guillotine.

This is great and dextrous translation and peerless nonsense.

LEWIS CARROLL

Jabberwocky

'Twas brillig, and the slithy toves
    Did gyre and gimble in the wabe:
All mimsy were the borogoves,
    And the mome raths outgrabe.

"Beware the Jabberwock, my son!
    The jaws that bite, the claws that catch!
Beware the Jubjub bird, and shun
    The frumious Bandersnatch!"

He took his vorpal sword in hand:
    Long time the manxome foe he sought—
So rested he by the Tumtum tree,
    And stood awhile in thought.

And, as in uffish thought he stood,
    The Jabberwock, with eyes of flame,
Came whiffling through the tulgey wood,
    And burbled as it came!

One, two! one, two! And through and through
    The vorpal blade went snicker-snack!
He left it dead, and with its head
    He went galumphing back.

"And hast thou slain the Jabberwock?
    Come to my arms, my beamish boy!
O frabjous day! Callooh! Callay!"
    He chortled in his joy.

'Twas brillig, and the slithy toves
    Did gyre and gimble in the wabe:
All mimsy were the borogoves,
    And the mome raths outgrabe.

Der Jammerwoch

Es brillig war. Die *schlichten* Toven
   Wirrten und wimmelten im Waben;
Und aller-mümsige Burggoven
   Die mohmen Räth' ausgraben.

Bewahre doch vor Jammerwoch!
   Die Zähne knirschen, Krallen kratzen!
Bewahr' vor Jub jub-Vogel, vor
   Frumiösen *Banderschnatzen*!

Er griff sein vorpals Schwertchen zu,
   Er suchte lang das manchsam' Ding;
Dann, stehend *unter'm* Tumtum Baum,
   Er an-zu-denken-fing.

Als stand er tief in Andacht auf,
   Des Jammerwochen's Augen-feuer
Durch tulgen Wald mit wiffeln kam,
   Ein burblend Ungeheuer!

Eins, Zwei! Eins, Zwei! Und durch und durch
   Sein vorpals Schwert zerschniferschnück,
Da blieb es todt! Er, Kopf in Hand,
   Geläumfig zog zurück!

Und schlugst Du ja den Jammerwoch?
   Umarme mich, mein Böhm'sches Kind!
O Freuden-Tag! O Halloo-Schlag!
   Er chortelt froh-gesinnt.

Es brillig war. Die *schlichten* Toven
   Wirrten und wimmelten im Waben;
Und aller-mümsige Burggoven
   Die mohmen Räth' ausgraben.

Translated by Dr. Robert Scott
("Thomas Chatterton")

Le Jaseroque

Il brilgue: les tôves lubricilleux
Se gyrent en vrillant dans le guave,
Enmimés sont les gougebosqueux,
Et le mômerade horsgrave.

Garde-toi du Jaseroque, mon fils!
La gueule qui mord; la griffe qui prend!
Garde-toi de l'oiseau Jube, évite
Le frumieux Band-à-prend.

Son glaive vorpal en main il va-
T-à la recherche du fauve manscant;
Puis arrivé à l'arbre Té-Té,
Il y reste, réfléchissant.

Pendant qu'il pense, tout uffusé
Le Jaseroque, à l'œil flambant,
Vient siblant par le bois tullegeais,
Et burbule en venant.

Un deux, un deux, par le milieu,
Le glaive vorpal fait pat-à-pan!
La bête défaite, avec sa tête,
Il rentre gallomphant.

As-tu tué le Jaseroque?
Viens à mon cœur, fils rayonnais!
O jour frabbejeais! Calleau! Callai!
Il cortule dans sa joie.

Il brilgue: les tôves lubricilleux
Se gyrent en vrillant dans le guave,
Enmimés sont les gougebosqueux
Et le mômerade horsgrave.

Translated by Frank L. Warrin, Jr.

ℭ ON A HOLIDAY AT DURHAM in the summer of 1855, Charles Lut-
widge Dodgson was staying at Whitburn with his cousins. They
were playing a rhyming game after dinner, composing nonsense
poetry in a kind of imaginary Anglo-Saxon, for which they were in-
venting the vocabulary. Young Charles's contribution to the human
race on that occasion was the first stanza of "Jabberwocky." He was
twenty-three that year.

Almost seventeen years later (we are told by his nephew), while
he was writing *Through the Looking-Glass* to follow *Alice*, he came
onto the little quatrain in one of his scrapbooks, and made a ballad
of it by adding five stanzas and the Jabberwock. During these years
which he spent at Oxford lecturing in mathematics, he had not only
written *Alice* and his works on Euclid, he had been ordained a dea-
con and had become a well-known photographer as well. When such
a man at forty finds that a piece of nonsense verse of his own, written
at twenty-three, is still worthy of him and still amusing, something is
bound to happen. Something did. The effect of "Jabberwocky" on
the *Alice* enthusiasts was immediate and electric.

It was only a matter of weeks before a German version appeared in
Macmillan's Magazine in a very funny letter to the editor from
"Thomas Chatterton," who had had it rapped out for him by a Ger-
man ghost, he said, at a spiritualistic seance. Shortly afterwards, how-
ever, his son confessed that "Thomas Chatterton" was really Dr.
Robert Scott, the distinguished classical scholar, formerly Master of
Balliol College, Oxford, and now Dean of Rochester, who had pro-
duced the translation overnight on a wager.

The German version in the text here is the original Macmillan
version—with the exception of the italicized words, which are corrected mistakes. Williams and Madan in *The Handbook of the Literature of the Rev. C. L. Dodgson (Lewis Carroll)* are responsible for
changing *schlichte* in the first line to *schlichten*, and *unten* in the seventh line, which is neither German nor nonsense, to *unter'm*, which is
both. But, somehow, Macmillan's *Banderschnätzchen* in the eighth
line, which should have been *Banderschnatzen*, seems to have been

overlooked. In the first place, the Bandersnatch is very big—almost as big as a dinosaur, for instance—and in the second, *Banderschnätzchen* does not rhyme with *kratzen*, which it must have done in the manuscript since all the other rhymes are impeccable. It is impossible to imagine that any of these errors could have been made by the learned Dr. Scott of Liddell and Scott's *Greek-English Lexicon*, who was a German scholar as well. They were made more probably by a muddled typesetter setting up the unfamiliar Gothic type in which the Macmillan version was printed.

Through the Looking-Glass, chiefly because of the insurmountable difficulties in the chess-playing parts, has never been attempted in any other language, and it was a very long time before anybody undertook the French "Jaseroque." Mr. Frank Lord Warrin, Jr.'s French translation appeared some sixty years after Dr. Scott's German one, in the *New Yorker* for Jan. 10, 1931, without a word of explanation or comment. His is probably the only French one there is.

I am sorry that the mathematician, Dodgson, and the lexicographer, Scott, who probably knew each other, were no longer alive when Mr. Warrin joined the distinguished company. They would have died of laughter to know that Mr. Warrin's contribution to English letters, outside of "Le Jaseroque," was *The Neutrality of Belgium*, a definitive document on the subject, published in 1918 by the United States Government Printing Office.

Both translations are in the spirit in which Carroll wrote his poem in the first place. That is to say, they were written for fun and for no other reason. It is possible that no other translations have ever been published either in Germany or France. It is even probable that these two have never been looked up by any French or German person. They seem to be for us.

Why is it—I find it interesting and amusing to wonder—that so much of the finest nonsense in English comes out of rectories and deaneries, where it springs (full panoplied) from the witty, gentle heads of clergymen? This is either very, very difficult to understand, or—and God forgive me—it isn't difficult at all!

GEOFFREY CHAUCER

Canterbury Tales
From the Prologue

Whan that Aprille with his shoures soote
The droghte of March hath perced to the roote,
And bathed every veyne in swich licour
Of which vertu engendred is the flour;
Whan Zephirus eek with his sweete breeth
Inspired hath in every holt and heeth
The tendre croppes, and the yonge sonne
Hath in the Ram his halve cours yronne,
And smale foweles maken melodye,
That slepen al the nyght with open yë •
(So priketh hem nature in hir corages),—
Thanne longen folk to goon pilgrimages,
And palmeres for to seken straunge strondes,
To ferne halwes, kowthe in sondry londes;
And specially from every shires ende
Of Engelond to Caunterbury they wende,
The hooly blisful martir for to seke
That hem hath holpen whan that they were seeke.

Die Canterbury-Erzählungen
From Der Allgemeine Prolog

Wenn der Aprilmond sanften Regen bringt,
Der Märzendürre an die Wurzel dringt,
Und jede Ader mit solch Säften schwellt,
Daß diese Kraft erzeugt die Blumenwelt,

Wenn Zephyr auch mit seinem süssen Hauch
Die zarten Trieb' in Heide, Wald und Strauch
Erweckt hat, und der jungen Sonne Brand
Des Widders Hälfte hat durchrannt,
Wenn lust'ge Melodie das Vöglein macht,
Das offnen Auges schläft die ganze Nacht
—So stachelt die Natur es in der Brust—:
Dann treibt das Volk die Wallfahrtslust
Und Pilger, fortzuziehn zu fremden Strande,
Zu fernen Heil'gen, kund in manchem Lande.
Besonders sieht man aus den Gauen allen
Von England sie nach Canterbury wallen
Dem segensreicher Märtyrer zum Dank,
Der ihnen half, als sie einst flech und krank.

Translated by Wilhelm Hertzberg

Les Contes de Canterbury

From Le Prologue

Quand Avril de ses averses douces
a percé la sécheresse de Mars jusqu'à la racine,
et baigné chaque veine de cette liqueur
par la vertu de qui est engendrée la fleur;
quand Zephyr aussi de sa douce haleine
a ranimé dans chaque bocage et bruyère
les tendres pousses, et que le jeune soleil
a dans le Bélier parcouru sa demi-course;
et quand les petits oiseaux font mélodie,
qui dorment toute la nuit l'œil ouvert,
(tant Nature les aiguillonne dans leur cœur),
alors ont les gens désirent d'aller en pèlerinage,
et les paumiers de gagner les rivages étrangers,
allant aux lointains sanctuaires, connus en divers pays;

et spécialement, du fond de tous les comtés
de l'Angleterre, vers Canterbury ils se dirigent,
pour chercher le saint et bienheureux martyr
qui leur a donné aide, quand ils étaient malades.

Translated by Louis Cazamian

꩜ DURING ALL THE YEARS that I have been repeating the Prologue
to the *Canterbury Tales* to myself, it has turned in my head into
a panel of wonderfully carved wood. The very words are oak.

In the carving the procession of storytellers, their cloaks and the
trappings of their horses still glowing with vestiges of medieval paint,
is a frieze in high relief crossing the panel from London to Canterbury. Behind these figures, in the Gothic trees that border the road,
the "smale foweles," much too big, are singing in the branches. Behind the trees, in low relief among his geometric fields, perhaps a
plowman, like a person in an almanac, stands to watch the pilgrims
passing in the road. On the left above the trees, carved rain slants
from a wooden cloud, and from another, on the right, young Zephirus
leans down and blows, his cheeks puffed out, his hands a trumpet at
his mouth, and in between them, gloriously over all, striking his
heraldic rays into the new-plowed earth, the "yonge sonne," bur-
nished gold, hangs in the Ram.

Both translations are distinguished and handsome. Both are modern—Professor Cazamian's made in 1908, Herr Harzberg's in 1925.
Neither has attempted a translation into the French or German of
Chaucer's time—which would have been fatal—but both have succeeded masterfully in preserving, in both modern languages, the special flavor of Chaucer's medieval, wooden words.

Here, by comparing the words in these three poems, is a splendid
opportunity to see how very closely related the three languages still
were in the fourteenth century.

SAMUEL TAYLOR COLERIDGE

Kubla Khan

In Xanadu did Kubla Khan
A stately pleasure-dome decree:
Where Alph, the sacred river ran
Through caverns measureless to man
   Down to a sunless sea.
So twice five miles of fertile ground
With walls and towers were girdled round:
And there were gardens bright with sinuous rills,
Where blossomed many an incense-bearing tree;
And here were forests ancient as the hills,
Enfolding sunny spots of greenery.

But oh! that deep romantic chasm which slanted
Down the green hill athwart a cedern cover!
A savage place! as holy and enchanted
As e'er beneath a waning moon was haunted
By woman wailing for her demon-lover!
   And from this chasm, with ceaseless turmoil seething,
As if this earth in fast thick pants were breathing,
A mighty fountain momently was forced:
Amid whose swift half-intermitted burst
Huge fragments vaulted like rebounding hail,
Or chaffy grain beneath the thresher's flail:
And 'mid these dancing rocks at once and ever
It flung up momently the sacred river.
Five miles meandering with a mazy motion
Through wood and dale the sacred river ran,
Then reached the caverns measureless to man,
And sank in tumult to a lifeless ocean:
and 'mid this tumult Kubla heard from far
Ancestral voices prophesying war!

The shadow of the dome of pleasure
Floated midway on the waves;
Where was heard the mingled measure
From the fountain and the caves.
It was a miracle of rare device,
A sunny pleasure-dome with caves of ice!

A damsel with a dulcimer
In a vision once I saw:
It was an Abyssinian maid,
And on her dulcimer she played,
Singing of Mount Abora.
Could I revive within me
Her symphony and song,
To such a deep delight 'twould win me,
That with music loud and long,
I would build that dome in air,
That sunny dome! those caves of ice!
And all who heard should see them there,
And all should cry, Beware! Beware!
His flashing eyes, his floating hair!
Weave a circle round him thrice,
And close your eyes with holy dread,
For he on honey-dew hath fed,
And drunk the milk of Paradise.

Kubla Khan

In Xanadu ließ Kubla Khan
Der Lust geräumigen Dom erstehen,
Wo Alph, das heilige Wasser, rann
Durch Höhlen ohne Maß und Plan
    Zu sonnenloser See.
Zehn Meilen so von Frucht und Grund

Umgürtet Wall und Mauerrund,
Die Gärten voll von Rinnsal vielgestalt,
Wo mit dem Laub von Weihrauch Bäume blühn,
Und schwarze Wälder, wie die Hügel alt,
Mit Sonnenflecken zwischen Immergrün.

Doch oh, durch grüne Hügel die romantische Schlucht,
Der tiefe Spalt quer unter Zedernhainen,
O wilde Stätte! Heilig und verflucht,
Wie jene, die ein Weib je heimgesucht,
Dem liebsten der Dämonen nachzuweinen.
Aus diesem Spalt, da wilder Aufruhr kochte,
Als ob die Erd in steten Stößen pochte,
Ohn Aufenthalt hoch eine Springflut sprang,
In deren heißem, ungestaltem Drang
Bruchstücke flogen, rückgeschnellt wie Hagel,
Und wie die Spreu sprühte von des Dreschers Schlegel.
In diesem Tanz der Brocken und Getrümmer
Sprang auf das heilige Wasser, jählings immer.
Fünf Meilen wandernd irren Wandelgang
Durch Wald und Tal das heilige Wasser rann,
Trat in die Höhlen ohne Maß und Plan,
Bis sprudelnd es ins starre Meer versank.
Und Kubla hörte aus den wilden Schlünden
Der Ahnen Stimme fern vom Kriege künden.

Des Freudendomes Schatten schwebte
Und spielte spiegelnd auf der Welle,
Da Rhythmus Rhythmus sich verwebte:
Der Höhlen Echo und der Quelle.
Ein seltner Plan und wundersam ersonnen:
Eisgrotten und der Dom der Lust voll Sonnen.

Ein Fräulein mit dem Harfenspiel,
Die einst im Traum ich sah;
Sie kam aus Abessinienland,
Schlug ihre Harfe mit der Hand
Und sang vom Berge Abora.

Strömt' wieder durch die Brust mir
Süß ihr Zusammenklang,
Steig' aus dem Sang Lust mir,
So daß mit Liedern laut und lang
In Luft ich ließ' den Dom erstehn,
Den Sonnendom! Das Eisverließ!
Und die mich hörten, würden sehn
Und rufen: Wunder! Wunderbar!
Sein Aug aus Blitz! Aus Sturm Sein Haar!
Schlingt dreifach einen Kreis um dies!
Schließt euer Aug vor heiliger Schau,
Denn er genoß vom Honig-Tau
Und trank die Milch vom Paradies.

Translated by Heinz Politzer

Kubla Khan

A Xanadu Kubla Khan ordonna
De bâtir un majestueux palais;
Là où coulait Alph, le fleuve sacré,
Par des grottes insondables à l'homme,
    Jusqu'à une mer sans soleil.
Donc dix mille pas de terrain fertile
De murs et de tours furent ceinturés;
En des jardins, brillants de sinueux ruisseaux,
Maint arbre fleurissait, tout chargé de parfums;
Et des forêts aussi anciennes que le monde
Entouraient des espaces vert ensoleillés.

Mais oh! le saisissant et le profond abîme
Qui tranchait la colline verte, sous les cèdres!
Lieu sauvage, aussi saint et aussi enchanté
Que ceux qu'a pu hauter, sous la lune au déclin,
Femme en pleurs appelant le démon, son amant!

Et de ce gouffre, qui bouillonnait sans répit,
Comme au souffle rapide et pesant de la terre,
Par moments jaillissait un torrent gigantesque;
Avec son jet, rapide et parfois suspendu,
De grands rocs bondissaient comme saute la grêle,
Ou la balle et le grain, sous les coups du fléau;
Et, mêlée à ces rocs en mouvement, le gouffre
Projetait par instants la rivière sacrée.
D'un lit tout en détours serpentant sur cinq lieues,
Elle courait dans les forêts et les vallons,
Puis atteignait les creux insondables à l'homme,
Tombant avec fracas en un océan mort;
Et dans ce bruit Kubla entendit, à distance,
Par d'ancestrales voix prophétiser la guerre!

L'image de ce palais de plaisir
Flottait sur l'onde au milieu du courant;
Là s'entendait la cadence mêlée
Qui venait de la source et des cavernes.
Tel était le succès d'un art miraculeux:
Un palais au soleil sur des grottes de glace!

Une demoiselle avec un tympanon
M'est apparue en un songe jadis;
C'était une vierge abyssinienne,
Et de son tympanon elle jouait,
Célébrant le mont Abora.
Si je pouvais faire renaître
En moi sa musique et son chant,
J'en serais rempli d'un si grand plaisir,
Qu'avec des accords sonores et longs
Je bâtirai ce palais dans les airs,
Ce palais au soleil! Ces creux de glace!
Et tous, m'écoutant, les apercevraient,
Et tous s'écrieraient: "Prenez, prenez garde!
A ses yeux de feu, ses cheveux flottants!
Autour de lui tracez trois fois un cercle,

Et ferme les yeux de sainte terreur,
Car il s'est nourri de rosée de miel,
Et du Paradis il a bu le lait."

Translated by Louis Cazamian

ℬ HERR POLITZER AND PROFESSOR CAZAMIAN have fulfilled their impressive tasks with profound understanding and a great reverence for Coleridge which is obvious at once. Here are two outstanding examples of fine translation.

The extraordinary circumstances under which the two existing fragments of *Kubla Khan* came to be are well known. Coleridge was literally enchanted when he dreamt them. His translators, on the other hand, were faced from start to finish not with dreams, primarily, but with almost insurmountable linguistic hazards. It is impossible to imagine how they managed these translations at all.

"Look," you will say, "how Coleridge's wonderful imagery is here, and how the 'sights and sounds' and the music of the dreaming words are here. And they are all of them in both!" You will say this after your first reading. "And all the blended portents of Paradise and impending Doom are balefully implicit in 'Der Ahnen Stimme fern vom Kriege künden,' and in 'Un palais au soleil sur des grottes de glace!' The meter and the changes in meter have been very delicately observed," you will say. "And the wonderful cool change in pace and instrumentation that introduces the second fragment is remarkably as it should be. The 'demoiselle avec un tympanon' and the 'Fräulein mit dem Harfenspiel' seem to me as breathtakingly beautiful as they were in English."

Even after your eighth, tenth, and twelfth readings you will still be saying, "The slowly rising nightmare warning with which the poem ends is marvelous!" and you will be right. I agree with you completely.

And don't you think, as I do, that these are fine poems in their own right, with something like the shadow of Coleridge himself coming through into both French and German?

Only one thing—the impossible, I suppose—is missing from them both. This is not apparent at once. I can say it only because I have read the poems so very much oftener than you have.

"Ad pulcritudinem tria requiruntur: integritas, consonantia, claritas," Aquinas said.

Both these translations are quite as remarkable to me now as they ever were for their "wholeness," and almost as remarkable for their "harmony," but a delicate sense of strain has taken the place of the "claritas"—which Joyce chooses to call "radiance." The translators' predicament is hopeless since with Coleridge the radiance struck first of all and the rest followed.

Must this fading "claritas" always be the forfeit exacted from a conscientious translator for daring to undertake a lyric poem that rhymes? I am so afraid it must.

E. E. CUMMINGS

"the hours rise up"

the hours rise up putting off stars and it is
dawn
into the street of the sky light walks scattering poems

on the earth a candle is
extinguished   the city
wakes
with a song upon her
mouth having death in her eyes

and it is dawn
the world
goes forth to murder dreams . . .

i see in the street where strong
men are digging bread
and i see the brutal faces of
people contented hideous hopeless cruel happy

and it is day,
in the mirror
i see a frail
man
dreaming
dreams
dreams in the mirror

and it
is dusk   on earth

a candle is lighted
and it is dark.
the people are in their houses

the frail man is in his bed
the city

sleeps with death upon her mouth having a song in her eyes
the hours descend
putting on stars . . .

in the street of the sky night walks scattering poems

"les heures se lévent"

les heures se lèvent éteignant les étoiles et voici
l'aube
dans la rue du ciel la lumiere en éparpillant des poèmes

sur la terre une chandelle est
éteinte   la ville
s'éveille
un chant sur sa
bouche la mort dans ses yeux

et voici l'aube
le mond
part pour assassiner des rêves . . .

je vois dans la rue où des hommes
forts piochent du pain
et je remarque les figures brutales des
gens contents hideux desespérés cruels heureux

et voici le jour,
dans la glace
je remarque un homme
frêle
rêvant
des rêves
des rêves dans la glace

et voici
le crépuscule   sur la terre

une chandelle est allumée
et il fait noir.
les gens sont chez eux
l'homme frêle est dans son lit
la ville

dort avec la mort dans sa bouche un chant dans ses yeux
les heures descendent
allumant les étoiles . . .

dans la rue du ciel la nuit marche en semant des poèmes

Translated by Eugéne Jolas

"die stunden steigen hinauf"

die stunden steigen hinauf sterne ablegend und es ist
morgen
in die straße dem himmel hinein geht das licht
                              gedichte streuend
auf der erde wird eine kerze
ausgelöscht   die stadt
erwacht
mit einem lied auf ihrem
mund als sie den tod in ihren augen hatte

und es ist morgen
die welt
geht hinaus träume zu morden . . .

ich sehe in der straße wo starke
männer brod graben
und ich sehe die thierische gesichter der
leute zufrieden abscheulich hoffnungslos grausam glücklich

und es ist der tag,
in dem spiegel
sehe ich einen gebrechlicher
mann
träume
träumen
träume im spiegel

und es
dämmert   auf der erde
wird eine kerze erleuchtet
und es ist dunkel.
die leute sind in ihren häusern
der gebrechlicher mann ist in seinem bett
die stadt

schläft mit dem tod auf ihrem mund als sie ein lied in
                              ihren augen hatte

die stunden steigen hinab
sterne anlegend ...

in der straße dem himmel geht die nacht
                    gedichte streuend

Translated by Victor Proetz

IF ONE WERE TO POUR A STREAM of sand from one hand into the
other slowly, and then slowly pour it back again, he would be
doing something in the form of this poem. It is a poem without ends
—not as a circle is endless, but as the figure 8 is endless. This is a
pleasant, quiet poem—except at first glance—and, in spite of its
craftsy, homemade look, Mr. Cummings has done a very subtle thing
with the rhyme. There is only one rhyme, and the rhyming words are
two sounds struck on a bell twelve hours apart. The echoes can be
sustained in the mind only because, under opposite circumstances,

they have been set into almost identical phrases, and the variation
is the rhyme.

> Into the street of the sky light walks . .
> in the street of the sky night walks . . .

This is a device for music. When a musical phrase is rhymed after a
long interval with a similar phrase with a single variation, the empha-
sis falls on the variation.

This delicate effect is possible only in English since "light" and
"night" happen to rhyme. Neither French nor German offers this
coincidence, and the choice of "lumière" and "nuit," "Licht" and
"Nacht," is inevitable since these words have no synonyms.

These beautifully balanced phrases of Cummings' can be made to
balance again, and so can the figure 8 be carried through both times.
So can his typographical mannerisms, which detract in neither language from the sound of the poem, although I have no idea how they
look to a French or German person.

CHARLES DICKENS

From **A Christmas Carol**

Marley was dead, to begin with. There was no doubt what-ever about that. The register of his burial was signed by the clergyman, the clerk, the undertaker, and the chief mourner. Scrooge signed it. And Scrooge's name was good upon 'Change, for anything he chose to put his hand to.

Old Marley was as dead as a door-nail.

Mind! I don't mean to say that I know, of my own knowledge, what there is particularly dead about a door-nail. I might have been inclined, myself, to regard a coffin-nail as the deadest piece of ironmongery in the trade. But the wisdom of our ancestors is in the simile; and my unhallowed hands shall not disturb it, or the Country's done for. You will therefore permit me to repeat, emphatically, that Marley was dead as a door-nail. . . .

[P. 9]

. . . . Bob, turning up his cuffs—as if, poor fellow, they were capable of being made more shabby—compounded some hot mixture in a jug with gin and lemons, and stirred it round and round and put it on the hob to simmer; Master Peter and the two ubiquitous young Cratchits went to fetch the goose, with which they soon returned in high procession.

Such a bustle ensued that you might have thought a goose the rarest of all birds; a feathered phenomenon, to which a black swan was a matter of course—and in truth it was something very like it in that house. Mrs. Cratchit made the gravy (ready beforehand in a little saucepan) hissing hot; Master Peter mashed the potatoes with incredible vigour; Miss Belinda sweetened up the apple-sauce; Martha dusted the hot plates; Rob took Tiny Tim beside him in a tiny corner at the table; the two young Cratchits set chairs for everybody, not forgetting themselves, and mounting guard upon their posts, crammed spoons into their mouths, lest they should shriek for goose before their turn came to be helped. At last the dishes were set on, and grace was said. It was succeeded by a breathless pause, as Mrs. Cratchit, looking slowly all along the carving-knife, prepared to plunge it in the breast; but when she did, and when the long expected gush of stuffing issued forth, one murmur of delight arose all around the board, and even Tiny Tim, excited by the two young Cratchits, beat on the table with the handle of his knife, and feebly cried Hurrah!

There never was such a goose. Bob said he didn't believe there ever was such a goose cooked. Its tenderness and flavour, size and cheapness, were themes of universal admiration. Eked out by apple-sauce and mashed potatoes, it was a sufficient dinner for the whole family; indeed, as Mrs. Cratchit said with great delight (surveying one small atom of a bone upon the dish), they hadn't ate it all at last! Yet every one had had enough, and the youngest Cratchits in particular, were steeped in sage and onion to the eyebrows! But now, the plates being changed by Miss Belinda, Mrs. Cratchit left the room alone—too nervous to bear witnesses—to take the pudding up and bring it in.

Suppose it should not be done enough! Suppose it should break in turning out! Suppose somebody should have got over the wall of the back-yard, and stolen it, while they were merry with the goose—a supposition at which the two young Cratchits became livid! All sorts of horrors were supposed.

Hallo! A great deal of steam! The pudding was out of the copper. A smell like a washing-day! That was the cloth. A smell like an eating-house and a pastrycook's next door to each other, with a laundress's next door to that! That was the pudding! In half a minute Mrs. Cratchit entered—flushed, but smiling proudly—with the pudding, like a speckled cannon-ball, so hard and firm, blazing in half of half-a-quartern of ignited brandy, and bedight with Christmas holly stuck into the top.

Oh, a wonderful pudding! Bob Cratchit said, and calmly too,

that he regarded it as the greatest success achieved by Mrs. Cratchit since their marriage. Mrs. Cratchit said that now the weight was off her mind, she would confess she had had her doubts about the quantity of flour. Everybody had something to say about it, but nobody said or thought it was at all a small pudding for a large family. It would have been flat heresy to do so. Any Cratchit would have blushed to hint at such a thing....

[Pp. 58–60]

Scrooge was better than his word. He did it all, and infinitely more; and to Tiny Tim, who did NOT die, he was a second father. He became as good a friend, as good a master, and as good a man, as the good old city knew, or any other good old city, town, or borough, in the good old world. Some people laughed to see the alteration in him, but he let them laugh, and little heeded them; for he was wise enough to know that nothing ever happened on this globe, for good, at which some people did not have their fill of laughter in the outset; and knowing that such as these would be blind anyway, he thought it quite as well that they should wrinkle up their eyes in grins, as have the malady in less attractive forms. His own heart laughed: and that was quite enough for him.

He had no further intercourse with Spirits, but lived upon the Total Abstinence Principle, ever afterwards; and it was always said of him, that he knew how to keep Christmas well, if any man alive possessed the knowledge. May that be truly said of us, and all of us! And so, as Tiny Tim observed, God bless Us, Every One!

[P. 97]

From Les apparitions de Noël

Marley était mort: pour commencer par le commencement. Il n'y a là-dessus aucun doute; le registre de son enterrement avait été signé par l'ecclésiastique, le sacristan, l'entrepreneur des funérailles et celui qui conduisait le deuil. Scrooge l'avait signé aussi, et le nom de Scrooge était une bonne signature à la Bourse sur tout papier où Scrooge l'apposait de sa main. Le vieux Marley était mort, bien mort! . . .

[The following paragraph is not translated into French.]

[P. 3]

Bob alors, relevant ses manches, prit un citron, et avec de l'extrait de genièvre il composa une sauce piquante, puis il dit à maître Pierre et aux deux jeunes Cratchit d'aller chercher l'oie. Ils revinrent bientôt en procession solonnelle.

A l'émotion qui s'empara de toute cette famille, vous auriez pu croire qu'une oie est le plus rare des volailles, un phénomène emplumé, auprès duquel un cygne noir serait un lieu commun. . . . Hélas! l'oie était réellement un oiseau rare dans cette maison. Mrs Cratchit fit chauffer le jus de ce beau rôti, maître Pierre acheva de peler les pommes de terre, miss Belinda mit du sucre dans la sauce aux pommes, Martha essuya les assiettes tièdes, Bob assit Tiny Tim près de lui à l'un des coins de la table, les deux petits Cratchit placèrent les chaises pour tout le monde sans s'oublier, et une fois à leur poste, se mirent leurs cuillers dans la bouche, de peur d'être tentés de demander de l'oie avant que vint leur tour d'être servis. Enfin la prière fut dite et il y eut un instant d'attente solennelle, lorsque Mrs Cratchit, promenant lentement son regard sur le couteau à découper, se prépara à le plonger dans les flancs de la bête, mais à peine l'eut-elle fait qu'un murmure de plaisir éclata autour d'elle: Tiny Tim lui-même, excité par les deux petits Cratchit, frappa sur la table avec le manche de son couteau et cria d'une voix faible: Hourra!

Jamais on ne vit oie pareille! Bob déclara qu'il ne croyait pas qu'on en eût jamais fait cuire une si grosse, si grasse, si tendre, si savoureuse et à si bon marché! Ce texte d'éloges fut commenté par l'admiration générale: avec la sauce aux pommes et les pommes de terre le dîner suffit à toute la famille. . . . "Et vraiment!" dit Mrs Cratchit à la vue d'un os resté dans le plat, "nous n'avons pas mangé tout!" Cependant chacun en avait en assez, et les petits Cratchit en particulier étaient bourrés de la garniture à la sauge et à l'oignon. Mais alors les assiettes étant changées par miss Belinda, Mrs Cratchit sortit seule . . . pour aller chercher le pouding!

Supposez qu'il soit manqué! supposez qu'il se brise quand on le tournera; supposez que quelqu'un ait sauté par-dessus le mur de la cour de derrière et l'ait volé pendant qu'un se régalait de l'oie. . . . A cette fatale supposition, les deux petits Cratchit devinrent blêmes! tout sortes d'horreurs furent supposées en une minute.

Mais quelle vapeur parfum . . . il approche. C'est lui, c'est le pouding porté par Mrs Cratchit, qui sourit toute glorieuse en regardant ce délicieux pouding, si ferme, si rond, semblable à un boulet de canon, noyé dans un quart de pinte d'eau-de-vie incandescente et décoré d'un petite branche du houx de Noël!

Oh! quel marveilleux pouding! Bob Cratchit déclara que c'était selon lui le chef-d'œuvre de Mrs Cratchit, le plus admirable pouding qu'elle eût fait depuis leur mariage. Mrs Cratchit répondit qu'a présent qu'elle n'avait plus ce souci sur la cœur, elle avouerait qu'elle avait en quelques doutes sur la quantité de farine: chacun eut un mot à dire; mais nul ne se permit de remarquer que c'était un bien petit pouding pour une si nombreuse famille. Il y aurait en blasphème à le penser. . . .

[Pp. 65–66]

Scrooge tint parole: il fit mieux, beaucoup mieux. Il fut un second père pour Tiny Tim, qui NE MEURAT PAS! il devint un bon ami, un bon maître, un bon homme, aussi bon qu'aucun marchand de la Cité, avant et depuis lui. Quelques personnes rirent de son changement; il les laissa rire, sachant bien qu'il vaut mieux rire que pleurer; il avait lui-même le rire au cœur: cela lui suffisait.

Il n'eut plus de commerce avec les Esprits; mais on disait de lui qu'il solennisait admirablement Noël: qu'on en dise autant de vous, de moi, de nous tous! et ainsi, comme s'exprimait Tiny Tim, "Dieu nous bénisse tous tant que nous sommes!"

[P. 112]

Translated by Amédée Pichot

From **Ein Weinachtslied in Prosa**

Marley war tot, damit beginnen wir. Jeglicher Zweifel hierüber ist ausgeschlossen. Sein Begräbsschein war vom Prediger, vom Küster, vom Leichenbesorger und von der wichtigsten der leidtragenen Personen unterschrieben worden. Schrooge unterschrieb gleichviel was er auch in die Hand nahm. Der alte Marley was tot, tot wie ein Türnagel.

Wohl verstanden! Es liegt nicht in meiner Absicht, sagen zu wollen, als wüßte ich aus meiner eigenen Kenntnis, was den gerade an einem Türnagel sonderlich Totes zu finden sei. Ich meinesteile hätte zu der Ansicht neigen mögen, als habe man einen Sargnagel als das toteste Stück Eisenware im Handel zu betrachten. Aber die Weisheit unsrer Ahnen ist in dem Gleichnis niedergelegt, und meine ungeweiten Hände sollen nicht daran rühren—sonst ist's um unser Vaterland geschen! Man wird mir deshalb gestatten, nachdrücklish zu wiederholen, daß Marley tot war, so tot wie ein Türnagel. . . .

[P. 7]

. . . und während Bob sich die Rockärmel aufkrempte—weil der Ärmste besorgte, sie möchten noch mehr abgenutzt werden und ein schäbigeres Außehen erhalten—und während er sich

eine heiße Bowle braute aus Wachholder und Zitronen, die er
emsig wieder und wieder umrührte und auf den Herd setzte,
daß sie zum Kochen käme; während Bob hiermit beschäftigt
war, ging der junge Herr Peter und die jungen Cratchits, die
beiden "Allgegenwärtigen," die beiden *"Hic et ubique"* aus, um
die Gans zu hohlen, mit der sie bald, in feierlichem Zuge
nahend, wiederkamen.

Nun folgte ein solches Gedränge, daß man hätte auf den
Gedanken kommen können, eine Gans sei der seltsamste Vogel
der Welt; ein geflügeltes Phänomenon, gegen das, ein raben-
schwarzer Schwan ein ganz natürliches Wesen sei—und so
verhielt es sich in Wahrheit auch bei Cratchits. Frau Cratchit
ließ die schon vorher in einem Tiegel zugerichtete Braten Sauce
sieden und wallen; der junge Herr Peter quetschte die Kar-
toffeln mit unglaublicher Kraftanstrengung; Fräulein Belinda
zuckerte die Apfelsauce; Martha putzte die geräumigen Teller;
Bob trug Tiny Tim nach einer gemütlichen Ecke am Tisch,
neben dem Platze den er selbst inne hatte; die beiden jungen
Cratchits setzten für jeden Stühle zurecht, wobei sie sich selbst
nicht vergaßen, und auf ihren Plätzen wachten sie über den
Bratprozeß und steckten die Löffel in den Mund, damit sie nicht
nach den Keulen schrien, ehe sie an die Reihe kämen. Endlich
wurde eine wahre Totenstille: während Frau Cratchit nach dem
Tranchiermesser Umschau hielt, in Bereitschaft, es der Gans
durch den Busen zu rennen. Als sie ihren Vorsatz nun aber zur
Ausführung brachte, als der heißersehnte Füllungsschwall her-
vorquoll, da erhob sich an der ganzen Tafel ein Gemurmel des
Entzückens, und selbst Tiny Tim, ermuntert durch die beiden
jungen Cratchits, schlug auf den Tisch mit dem Griff seines
Messers und rief mit schwacher Stimme: "Hurra!"

Nie ward eine solche Gans gesehen! Bob sagte, er glaube
nicht, daß jemals eine solche Gans gebraten worden sei. Ihre
Zartheit und ihr Duft, ihre Größe und ihre Billigkeit gaben
Stoß zu allgemeiner und inniger Bewunderung. Mit dem Zusatz
von Apfelsauce und Kartoffelmus gab sie ein reichliches Mittag
für die ganze Familie ab; ja Frau Cratchit bemerkte sogar mit

großem Erzücken (als sie ein kleines Knöchelchen noch auf
der Schüssel liegen sah), sie hätten zu guter Letzt noch nicht
einmal alles aufgegessen! Aber doch hatte jeder reichlich
gehabt, und ganz besonders die jüngsten Cratchits; bis über die
Ohren waren sie voll Salbei und Zwiebeln! Aber als jetzt die
Teller von Fräulein Belinda gewechselt worden waren, da
verließ Frau Cratchit, um den Pudding aus der Pfanne zu
nehmen und hereinzutragen, das Zimmer—allein, denn sie war
zu eifrig und erregt, einen Begleiter zu dulden!

O, wenn er noch nicht gut genug wäre! wenn er etwa zer-
bräche beim Umwenden! Wenn gar jemand über die Hofmauer
geklettert wäre und ihm gestohlen hätte, während sie sich an
der Gans ergötzten—eine Besorgnis, bei der die jungen
Cratchits bleich wurden wie die Wand! Alles mögliche Entset-
zen wurde dergestalt in potentiale, hypothetische Satzgefüge
geschachtelt.

Hallo! Eine große Wolke Rauch und Dampf! Der Pudding
war aus dem Kessel gekippt worden. Nun ein Duft, wie an
einem Waschtage, der von der Serviette kam! Ein Duft wie aus
einem Speisehause und einer Kuchenbäckerei, die Tür an Tür
liegen neben der Tür eines Wäscheladens! Der kam vom Pudding! Im nächsten Augenblick kam Frau Cratchit herein—rot
wie ein Klatschmohn, aber mit einem stolzen Lächeln auf dem
Antlitz—mit dem Pudding, jener gelockten Kanonenkugel, so
prall und so fest, flammend in einem Achtelnössel glühenden
Rums, und geziert mit dem Stechginsterzweig, der oben drin
steckte.

O, wundervoller Pudding! Bob Cratchit sagte, und zwar ganz
still und ruhig sagte er es, er hielte diesen Pudding für das
hervorragendste, was Frau Cratchit seit ihrer Hochzeit gefertigt
habe. Frau Cratchit sagte, da nun der Stein von ihrem Herzen
genommen sei, müsste sie schon gestehen, daß ihr wegen des
Mehls gewaltig Angst und Bange gewesen wäre. Jeder hatte
etwas über den Pudding zu sagen, aber niemand sagte oder
dachte, daß es doch alles in allem ein kleiner Pudding sei für
eine so große Familie! Schale Ketzerei wäre sie gewesen, wenn

das jemand hätte tun wollen. Anny [*sic*] Cratchit würde sich über und über und über geschämt haben, hätte sie das auch leise andenken mögen. . . .

[Pp. 72–74]

Scrooge hielt sein Wort ehrlich. Er vollführte alles, was er versprach, und noch unendlich viel mehr; und dem kleinen Tiny Tim der NICHT starb, ward er zu einem zweiten Vater. Er wurde ein so guter Mensch, wie ihn die gute alte Altstadt, Stadt oder Vorstadt in der guten alten Welt nur jemals gekannt hat. Es gab ja Leute, die über die Veränderung, die sie mit ihm vorgehen sahen, lachten; aber er ließ sie lachen und gab wenig Acht darauf, denn er war weise genug zu wissen, daß nichts sich jemals zum guten ereignet auf dieser Erdkugel, vorüber nicht manche Leute aus vollem Halse lachen zu müssen meinen; und da er wußte, daß Leute solchen Schlages doch auf alle Fälle blind bleiben würden, meinte er, es sei ganz ebenso gut, wenn sich ihre Augen herbei verschrumpften, als wenn es weniger nett infolge von Krankheit geschähe. Ihm lachte das Herz im Leibe, und das genügte ihm!

Er hat mit Geistern keinen weiteren Umgang mehr gehabt, sondern hat hinfort streng dem Grundsatz gänzlicher Enthaltsamkeit gelebt; und immer hieß es von ihm, daß er Weihnachten richtig zu feiern wisse, wenn es irgend jemand bei Lebzeiten beschert sei, zu wissen, wie man Weihnachten feiern soll! Möge gleichens in Wahrheit von uns, und von uns allen, gesagt werden! Und darum, wie Tiny Tim sagte: "Schenk uns der liebe Gott deinen Segen! uns und allen andern Menschen!"

[P. 124]

Translated by Paul Heichen

℘ THIS TERRIBLE, WONDERFUL MASTERPIECE is in the style and taste of a Victorian whatnot, loaded to the breaking point with walnut veneer, mock gilding, sentimentality, and spoolwork. It is almost incredibly old-fashioned, stuffy beyond belief, and, in many little irritating ways, cheap at half the price. If Dickens had been paid by the word—and I could never quite believe in the rumor that he had been—he should have made himself a very pretty penny with this story, which, according to Andrew Lang, he failed to do.

In the opening paragraphs—probably the most famous and boring paragraphs in English literature—only two ideas that are needed for the story are swamped in yards and yards of the most relentless machine carving. Marley was dead, is one of them; Scrooge's name was good for anything, is the other. But something else is there. "Old Marley was as dead as a door-nail" is there, and that is the best-known sentence in the whole story. The magic begins with that sentence. Nobody knows why but, whenever the *Christmas Carol* is mentioned, everybody in the room will think of that sentence at once.

The magic of the *Christmas Carol* is no ordinary magic. There is nothing frightening or supernatural about the ghosts at all. All three of them are perfectly opaque and are only trumped-up, allegorical, papier-mâché dummies fifteen feet high, with stagehands inside them, rolling them around. Dickens' magic is of quite another kind. His is the magic of the Cratchits' Christmas, which is incomparable in English and so definitively the greatest Christmas we have that it is impossible not to think of it whenever one is reading about any of the others—Joyce's at the Misses Morkan's in "The Dead," for instance, or Dylan Thomas' in the "Child's Christmas in Wales."

The difference between Herr Heichen, the German translator, and M. Pichot, the French one, is that Herr Heichen loved his work and would have died for Mr. Dickens, while M. Pichot didn't and would not have. As a result, Herr Heichen has given us very convincingly British, Camden Town Cratchits, speaking a kind of Cockney German, while M. Pichot comes through with some two-dimensional French people who live, very unconvincingly, somewhere behind the Gare du Nord, maybe, where nobody ever goes.

Herr Heichen is charming. He is so carried away that in his blind enthusiasm he frequently finds himself adding a few irresistible little wooden rosettes of his own to the Master's. Not only does Tiny Tim become "kleiner Tiny Tim" at one exciting point, but an extra member is suddenly added to the family when "Any Cratchit would have blushed . . ." becomes in German "Anny Cratchit would have been ashamed of herself over and over and over again . . ." But never mind. Herr Heichen has managed to produce a conscientious German whatnot in precisely the right style. He has written a very good story.

M. Pichot hasn't. M. Pichot has given his translation the clipping an English sheep dog might be given in an attempt to make an impossible poodle of him. He has chucked out shovelfuls of the Master's scrolls without a qualm. Mustn't he have known he was being disrespectful when he didn't bother to translate the famous "dead-as-a-door-nail" paragraph *at all*? And look what a mess he's made of the end! Was he perfectly irresponsible? (Can he have been a relative of the publisher's?)

Oh, M. Pichot! You didn't like Dickens, did you? Some people don't. And you were never told, were you, that it is customary in all civilized English-speaking places to read every word of the *Christmas Carol* aloud every year on Christmas Eve, with even the youngest members of the family sitting "round the hearth, in what Bob Cratchit called a circle, meaning half a one," in their little red dressing gowns? I thought not.

I wouldn't dream of telling you that when she read this, one of them said, "*Please*, Grandfather, not *every* year!"

EMILY DICKINSON

"I lost a world the other day"

I lost a world the other day.
Has anybody found?
You'll know it by the row of stars
Around its forehead bound.

A rich man might not notice it;
Yet to my frugal eye
Of more esteem than ducats.
Oh, find it, sir, for me!

"J'ai perdu, l'autre jour, un monde"

J'ai perdu, l'autre jour, un monde:
Quelqu'un l'aurait-il retrouvé?
Un rang d'étoiles, à la ronde,
Autour de son front est lové.

Un riche n'en aurait point cure,
Mais pour mes économes yeux
Je vaut de l'or—avec usure:
Retrouvez-le pour moi, Monsieur!

Translated by Fernand Baldensperger

"Neulich verlor ich eine Welt"

Neulich verlor ich eine Welt.
Hat irgend Jemand 'funden?

Man kennt sie von der Sternenreih'
Um ihre Stirn gebunden.

Ein Reicher merkt vielleicht es nicht,
In meiner einfach Sitte,
Mein Herr, mehr wie Dukaten, Werth.
O, finde sie mir, bitte!

Translated by Victor Proetz

I FEEL ALMOST SURE that in public life Miss Emily Dickinson was one of the daughters of Edward Dickinson, Esq., and Mrs. Dickinson of Amherst, Massachusetts, and nothing more. In private life, with the door closed, I believe that she thought of herself always as a poet—as an *undeniable* poet but as an *amateur* poet—and that, so far as her own wishes were concerned, was certainly enough. Emily Dickinson is not unlike one of those very exciting lesser painters whose sketchbooks are fabulous and whose finished paintings are not quite fabulous. She was an extraordinarily talented New England woman who liked terribly to invent poems and to write them down. I am not sure that she liked quite so much to read them after they were written.

What must have delighted her most to feel about herself, there, in the middle of the nineteenth century, in the security of Amherst and her little room, was that there would always be more poems than she could ever possibly write down, crowding each other out of her mind. And so, to keep from exploding with excitement, she scribbled everything at breakneck speed, whether it was a poem or not, as though she were making watercolor sketches that had to be finished before the paper dried. Many of her verses sound as though she might have been a little bit too tired to listen any longer to what was still bubbling out of her head, but since nobody else was meant to hear, she allowed her private grammar to run away with her—and why not?—in the way that a pianist allows himself to play wrong notes when he is playing something new, just for himself, and batting it out faster than he can think because, in his enthusiasm, he can't wait to hear how the thing goes.

After her death in 1886, a few of her finished poems were published, respectfully enough, with tenderness and discretion, by her sister Lavinia. And surely that was meant to be the end of it. Luckily —up to a point—for us, it was not the end at all.

It was not until fifty years after her death that Emily Dickinson became immortal—overnight, so to speak. She was suddenly "put over"—and I can't remember quite how it was done—by her niece (less tender and more canny than her aunt Lavinia had been), and some others, as a kind of posthumous prodigy. Everybody loved her at once for a variety of the damndest reasons, and everybody began saying and writing all sorts of things about her. Some enthusiasts mistook her style for a special outcropping of the kind of slovenly free verse that was being written at the time, and began thinking of her poems as the best of it. Others began comparing her epigrams to Goethe's. Still others called her the greatest woman poet since Sappho—but criticized her grammar. For a while there, a great many people were all talking about her at once and being very flighty indeed. People began dancing to her poems. People were all losing their heads.

Later on, years later, after some more quiet opinions had been allowed to mellow, Miss Dickinson of Amherst reminded people less and less of the twenties, since nothing in her writing was either self-conscious or arty, and none of her verse was properly "free verse." It was admitted that her epigrams resembled Goethe's only superficially, because they *were* epigrams rather than for any other reason. It became apparent that her grammatical mistakes were not exactly affectations. They were there only because she never bothered to correct experiments once she had tried them out on paper and rejected them. People began to agree that in ordinary, everyday speech, it would probably never have occurred to the daughter of the Treasurer of Amherst College to use "found" as an intransitive verb any more than she would habitually have talked baby-talk.

As to the nonsense about Sappho, it is all very well for anybody to think of Emily Dickinson as a second Sappho in the privacy of his own head—in case he doesn't mind thinking just anything that comes along—but saying it is silly and writing it down for all of us to read again and again, as it crops up in preface after preface of her poems, is unfair to Emily Dickinson, and impertinent. Emily Dickinson is not the *second* anything. Besides, if she were any Sappho at all, wouldn't she have had to be about the eighth? Aren't Clémence Isaure (c. 1450–1500), the Sappho of Toulouse; Mlle. Scudéry (1607–1701), the French Sappho; Catherine Cockburn (1679–1749), the Scotch Sappho; Lady Mary Wortley Montague (1689–1762), Alexander Pope's candidate; Mrs. Mary D. Robinson ("Perdita"), (1758–1800), George IV's candidate; and Mrs. Sarah Wentworth Morton (1759–1846), the American Sappho,* all ahead of her? Or aren't these eminent ladies required to line up?

Somehow, there will always be a few of us on hand to say that Stockholm is the Venice of the North (when it certainly used to be St. Petersburg—or even Amsterdam), and that Gladstone is the Napoleon of oratory, and that Voltaire is the Plato of the eighteenth century, and that Auden's is now the prescribed period style of the fifties. "Poor Queen Matilda!" I cannot help sighing, "if you only had —instead of hadn't—embroidered the Bayeux Tapestry, you might have been the Betsy Ross of the sixties (of the ten-sixties, I mean to say), or even the Sappho of needlework!"

Sappho, indeed!

I may know how this kind of thing happens. For instance:

At my first reading of Mr. Baldensperger's very nice French version of this little poem, I was unaccountably reminded of:

> C'était, dans la nuit brune,
> Sur la clocher jauni
>   La lune,
> Comme un point sur un i.

"Ah!" I might have cried—but didn't—"Emily Dickinson in French is now the second Alfred de Musset!" Wouldn't that have been something to *write down*?

---

* *The Reader's Encyclopedia,* edited by William Rose Benét (New York: Thomas Y. Crowell Company, 1948). See "Sappho."

My own slightly cast-iron translation into German carries through the highly special Dickinsonian intransitive " 'funden," at the expense of almost everything else. The result is a little poem in a kind of housemaid's German which I hope will not mislead any German scholars into stumbling into the notion that Emily Dickinson wrote in a New England dialect that flourished around Amherst. Besides, I had better say to them, Emily Dickinson must never be judged on the strength of any *one* of her poems.

T. S. ELIOT

Sweeney among the Nightingales

Apeneck Sweeney spreads his knees
Letting his arms hang down to laugh,
The zebra stripes along his jaw
Swelling to maculate giraffe.

The circles of the stormy moon
Slide westward toward the River Plate,
Death and the Raven drift above
And Sweeney guards the hornèd gate.

Gloomy Orion and the Dog
Are veiled; and hushed the shrunken seas;
The person in the Spanish cape
Tries to sit on Sweeney's knees

Slips and pulls the table cloth
Overturns a coffee-cup,
Reorganised upon the floor
She yawns and draws a stocking up;

The silent man in mocha brown
Sprawls at the window-sill and gapes;
The waiter brings in oranges
Bananas figs and hothouse grapes;

The silent vertebrate in brown
Contracts and concentrates, withdraws;
Rachel *née* Rabinovitch
Tears at the grapes with murderous paws;

She and the lady in the cape
Are suspect, thought to be in league;
Therefore the man with heavy eyes
Declines the gambit, shows fatigue,

Leaves the room and reappears
Outside the window, leaning in,
Branches of wistaria
Circumscribe a golden grin;

The host with someone indistinct
Converses at the door apart,
The nightingales are singing near
The Convent of the Sacred Heart,

And sang within the bloody wood
When Agamemnon cried aloud,
And let their liquid siftings fall
To stain the stiff dishonored shroud.

Sweeney parmi les rossignols

Sweeney-outang déploie ses jambes
Et, laissant choir ses bras, s'esclaffe;
Les stries qui zèbrent ses mâchoires
S'enflent en taches de girafe.

La lune d'orange dérive
Vers l'Occident et Santa-Fé
Aux nues la Mort, le Corbeau planent,
Sweeney défend l'Huis encorné.

Orion s'enténèbre, et le Chien;
Les mers contractées font silence;
La personne en cape espagnole
Gravit les genoux Sweeneyens

Trébuche, s'accroche à la nappe,
Fait culbuter la cafetière,
Et puis se recompose au sol
En remontant sa jarretière.

Le muet en veston moka
Se vautre à la fenêtre et bée;
Le garçon passe des sorbets
Des raisins et des ananas;

Le vertébré silencieux
Se ressaisit, bat en retraite
Tandis que Rachel née Nathan
Mord dans la pulpe à belles dents.

Trouvent ces deux dames suspectes,
Flairant entre elles quelque ligue,
L'homme aux yeux lourds refuse net
Le gambit, avoue sa fatigue,

Quitte la pièce et reparaît
À la fenêtre où il s'incline,
Inscrivant son rictus doré
Dans les rameaux d'une glycine;

Le patron confabule avec
Un quelconque interlocuteur
Qu'on ne voit; les rossignols chantent
Près du couvent du Sacré-Cœur,

Comme ils chantaient au bois sanglant
Lorsque râla Roi d'Argos,
Souillant de leurs fientes liquides
Le suaire raidi d'approbre.

Translated by Pierre Leyris

TO ME "Sweeney Among the Nightingales" is like a brilliantly slapdash painting in which impressions paint themselves in before your very eyes as you read. When the poem is over the painting is finished and there it is—all of it—still quivering and still wet. And it seems to me that M. Leyris understands all this. With the same wit he virtually paints Mr. Eliot's painting over again in virtually the same style. Since all the details have been splashed in at top speed —or seem to have been—it doesn't matter whether a well-aimed brush stroke stands for a banana or a pineapple or a stocking or a garter.

DANIEL DECATUR EMMETT

"DIXIE," LIKE "Yankee Doodle," has to do with a very amusing, durable tune and some not very amusing, fairly negligible words. Unlike "Yankee Doodle" the words and music were composed simultaneously during the course of a frenzied Sunday afternoon in 1859.

How it came to be batted out—in New York—to be used as a "walk-around" by Jerry Bryant's minstrels the next night, how it came to be played two years later at Jefferson Davis' presidential inauguration—in Montgomery, Alabama—and how, consequently, it came to be the Confederacy's "anthem," is all recorded in Charles Burleigh Galbraeth's *Daniel Decatur Emmett, Author of "Dixie."*

Europe knows the tune perfectly well—it turns up in any number of German and French medleys—but it doesn't know the words, I'm afraid. Frankly, neither do I. I just whistle along with everybody else, exactly as you are meant to do.

STEPHEN FOSTER

IN *Larousse de XXe Siècle* Stephen Foster is described as a "chansonnier populaire américain" with 125 "romances sentimentales, ou chansonnettes comiques" to his credit. *Meyers Lexikon* calls him a poet and composer of *Lieder und Balladen* "in einem unrechten Negerenglisch." *Larousse* and *Der Große Brockhaus* list his best-known songs with their titles in English, which makes me think that even though these are perfectly well known in France and Germany, they are probably sung in English.

It would have been more fun, of course, to have discovered references to things like "Hannchen mit dem hellbraunen Haar," or even "Vieux Joe noir." I would love to have come up with something *in einem unrechten Negerdeutsch.*

W. S. GILBERT

The Mikado

Act I. No. 6

Chorus.   Comes a train of little ladies
From scholastic trammels free;
Each a little bit afraid is,
Wond'ring what the world can be.
Is it but a world of trouble,
   Sadness set to song?
Is its beauty but a bubble
   Bound to break ere long?

Are the palaces and pleasures
   Fantasies that fade?
And the glory of its treasures
   Shadow of a shade?
And the glory of its treasures
   Shadow of a shade?
   Shadow of a shade?

School-girls we, eighteen and under,
From scholastic trammels free,
And we wonder—how we wonder!—
And we wonder—how we wonder!—
What on earth the world can be!
What on earth the world can be!

No. 7

Three little maids from school are we,
Pert as a school-girl well can be,
Fill'd to the brim with girlish glee,
   Three little maids from school.

Yum-Yum.   Ev'rything a source of fun.

Peep-Bo.	Nobody's safe, for we care for none!
Pitti-Sing.	Life is a joke that's just begun!
The Three.	Three little maids from school.
	Three little maids who, all unwary,
	Come from a ladies' seminary,
	Freed from its genius tutelary,
	Three little maids from school,
	Three little maids from school!
Yum-Yum.	One little maid is a bride, Yum-Yum—
Peep-Bo.	Two little maids in attendance come—
Pitti-Sing.	Three little maids is the total sum—
The Three.	Three little maids from school.
Yum-Yum.	From three little maids take one away—
Peep-Bo.	Two little maids remain, and they—
Pitti-Sing.	Won't have to wait very long, they say—
The Three.	Three little maids from school!
Chorus of Girls.	Three little maids from school.
Full Chorus.	Three little maids who, all unwary,
	Come from a ladies' seminary,
	Freed from its genius tutelary,
	Three little maids from school,
	Three little maids from school!

Der Mikado

Erster Akt. 8. Auftritt

Chor.	Kommt ein Mädchenzug gegangen
	Von dem läst'gen Schulzwang frei,
	In der Brust ein wenig Bangen
	Wundert was die Welt wohl sei!
	Wird wohl da in gleichem Masse
	Nur geweint? Geschwatzt?
	Ist was schön nur Seifenblase,
	Die gar bald geplatzt?

Sind die Schlösser, sind die Freuden
Leere Phantasien?
Und die Schätze Herrlichkeiten
Schatten, die verzieh'n?
Schatten, die verzieh'n?

Mädchen, achtzehn Jahr und drunter
Von dem läst'gen Schulzwang frei;
Und es nimmt uns schrecklich Wunder,
Was die Welt wohl sei!
Was die Welt wohl sei!

Trio: Yum-Yum, Piep-Bo, und Pitti-Sing.

Die Drei.	Drei kleine Mädchen vom Institute,
	Backfischchen wir, mit frohem Muth,
	Voll bis oben von Übermuth,
	Drei kleine Mädchen wir.
Yum-Yum.	Alles ist uns ein Quell der Lust!
Piep-Bo.	Und der Schelm sitzt in unserer Brust!
Pitti-Sing.	's Leben ist ein Scherz, der beginnt uns just!
Die Drei.	Drei kleine Mädchen wir!
	Drei kleine Mädchen unbesonnen,
	Nun der Schule Zwang entronnen,
	Und das Leben erst begonnen,
	Drei kleine Mädchen wir,
	Drei kleine Mädchen wir!
Yum-Yum.	Die eine Maid ist 'n Braut, Yum-Yum—
Piep-Bo.	Zwei sind Brautjungfern eben d'rum—
Pitti-Sing.	Drei kleine Mädchen die ganze Summ'—
Die Drei.	Drei kleine Mädchen wir.
Yum-Yum.	Nehmt eine Maid von dem Dreigespann—
Piep-Bo.	Zwei verbleiben und die, sagt man—
Pitti-Sing.	Brauchen nicht lange zu warten dann—
Die Drei.	Drei kleine Mädchen wir!
Chor.	Drei kleine Mädchen wir!

Alle.   Drei kleine Mädchen unbesonnen,
                 Nun der Schule Zwang entronnen,
                 Und das Leben erst begonnen,
                 Drei kleine Mädchen wir,
                 Drei kleine Mädchen wir!

                                   Translated by Ernest F. L. Gauss

ORDINARILY, ON SATURDAY AFTERNOONS in winter, when you were a child, you could skate in the Park, make a plant stick for your grandmother's birthday, repair your bicycle tire or, maybe, go to the Museum of Natural History with your father. Extraordinarily, on Saturday afternoons in winter, you were taken to see *The Mikado* with hot chocolate and a meringue glacé at the Plaza afterwards.

The Savoyards' first performance of *The Mikado* was on October 9, 1884, and the English text here is from the score as it was published in London the following year.

For some reason that isn't clear to me, its first performance in German was given in New York on February 13, 1886, and its second performance in German was given in Chicago in March a year later. Unless *The Mikado* was part of the repertoire of a touring German opera company, I cannot imagine why in America it would have been given in German at all. The second possibility is, of course, that these productions were by amateur German singing societies, of which there were still many in the Eighties.

The German text I have here—Ernest F. L. Gauss's translation— is very probably the one used on both these occasions. I have it from a dilapidated old paper-bound libretto that was printed to be sold in theater lobbies.

A friend of mine—an American woman—who, as a child, was taken to a performance of *The Mikado* in Berlin, has never forgotten

Drei kleine Mädchen, zuckergute,
Von einer Dameninstitute

which is probably from the second German translation by F. Zell and

R. Genée, which I have never seen. Theirs was the one used for the first performances in Vienna on March 2, 1888, and in Berlin on the sixth of the following December.

Alfred Loewenberg, in his *Annals of Opera, 1597–1940* (Geneva: Societas Bibliographica, 1955), records *The Mikado* as having been presented at Brussels on December 23, 1889, with a French libretto by M. Kafferath. This translation, unfortunately, is not available. Even the Library of Congress thinks this must be an unpublished manuscript. I have found nothing more except an undated newspaper clipping which records another performance in French at Calais. M. Loewenberg says *The Mikado* was "apparently never given in Paris," and this is probably true if he means "never given in French." Another friend of mine—a Frenchman this time—has seen *The Mikado* in Paris, "where," he tells me, "it is traditional to sing it in English." I wonder if it can't have been quite simply the D'Oyly Cartes that he has seen in Paris.

THOMAS JEFFERSON

The Constitution of the United States

(From the Preamble)

We the People of the United States, in Order to form a more perfect Union, establish Justice, insure domestic Tranquility, provide for the common defense, promote the general Welfare, and secure the Blessings of Liberty to ourselves and our Posterity, do ordain and establish this Constitution for the United States of America.

La Constitution des États-Unis

(From the Preamble)

Nous, le peuple des États-Unis, afin de former une union plus parfaite, d'établir la justice, d'assurer la tranquillité interieure, de pourvoir à la défense commune, d'accroître le bien-être général, et de rendre durables, pour nous comme pour notre postérité, les bienfaits de la liberté, nous faisons, nous décrétons et nous établissons cette constitution pour les États-Unis d'Amerique.

Translated by Thomas Jefferson

Die Verfassung der Vereinigten Staaten

(From the Preamble)

Wir, das Volk der Vereinigten Staaten, um eine vollkomene Vereinigung herbeizuführen, Gerechtigkeit festzustellen, innere

Ruhe zu sichern, für gemeinsame Wehr zu sorgen, allgemeine Wohlfart zu förden und den Segen der Freiheit uns und unsern Nachkommen zu erhalten, beschliessen und verfügen diese Verfassung für die Vereinigten Staaten von Amerika.

Translated by Dr. G. A. Zimmermann

ℭ IN TEXAS ONE SATURDAY AFTERNOON I found myself idle and went round to the Houston Public Library to see what of what I needed was to be found there. Part of the building had been closed off. The main reading room was being air-conditioned and I was directed to a reading room temporarily set up in a far wing beyond the stacks. On the way through I was confronted by an entire wall of German books. Since I had the whole afternoon ahead of me I began systematically with *A*, looking at the back of every book and making notes for another time, until I got to *Z*. It was there I discovered Dr. Zimmermann's *Vier Hundert Jahre Amerikanischer Geschichte*.

This is one of those old-fashioned red-and-gold-looking books with covers embossed in the style of the old bound volumes of *St. Nicholas*. It had been little used, judging from the freshness of the binding. There, in Dr. Zimmerman's appendix, was my first German Constitution of the United States. I had not got quite round to thinking about the Constitution. It was a little too soon; I wasn't ready for it. I was still at work on the people called *B*. The official translation, I was certain, would be somewhere else, but since I had it there, I copied out his Preamble.

Then some time elapsed.

At a party in New York the following winter, there was a young English woman I had not met before. She was sitting on a sofa with some friends of mine who were drinking whiskey and discussing old times and the Eighteenth Amendment. She couldn't be having a very good time, I thought.

"Come with me. We will talk about something else," I said to her, "something you know about."

"What do you mean? I studied the history of the United States at school, of course. I know all about the Constitution. Would you like to hear the Preamble? She closed her eyes to think for a moment. "*Nous, le peuple des États-Unis*—" she began.

"Do you mean," I said when she had finished it, "that you were taught American history in French?"

"Yes, of course."

"Why?"

"Because I was at school in France."

"And whose translation is that one, do you suppose?"

"I don't remember. Thomas Jefferson's, probably."

So I began looking for that—I had never heard of such a thing before—and after a while I found it. I found it twice—once in Beck's *La Constitution des États-Unis* at the New York Public Library, and again in Conseil's *Mélanges politiques et philosophiques extraits des Mémoires et de la correspondance de Thomas Jefferson* in Yale's Franklin Library.

"Of course, I've been doing it the hard way," I said later, telling these complications to a member of President Eisenhower's Cabinet and a member of the State Department. "There must be an easier way than this."

"Didn't it occur to you to write to the Government Printing Office?" said the Cabinet Member.

"They would have sent you hundreds of little blue pamphlets of the Constitution translated into every language in the world at ten cents a piece," added a newspaper editor who happened to be standing there.

"I wish I had thought of that. I'm sure you're right."

"I'm not," said the diplomat, "not a bit sure."

"Let's find out. Let's try it." I was very enthusiastic. "Who will write the letter? Will you, or will you?"

"You'll have to do that," they said between them, and they added something about my rights as a citizen. I sent off two identical letters, one to the United States Government Printing Office, the other to the Library of Congress.

Gentlemen:

Does the Government Printing Office issue official translations into foreign languages of the Constitution of the United States? If so, will you please advise me where and to whom to apply for a French and German one? If not, can you tell me where to find what may be considered the standard translations?

That was the letter.

Both replies came back very promptly. The Printing Office returned my letter to me with pencil notes in the margin. "Not available from this office" was written after "translations into foreign languages," and "No information available" was the answer to where to find the standard translations. There was a printed slip of green paper enclosed thanking me for my inquiry.

Mr. Henry J. Dubester of the Library of Congress was kind enough to provide me with five references which I am very happy to be able to include in the list. To my great amazement all of his are as obscure as mine. The New York Public Library, for instance, has neither Friese nor Lowenstein.

While I was awaiting these replies I thought of one thing more. I remembered that there was a bookstore in one of the United Nations buildings.

"No, sir," said a clerk, "we wouldn't be carrying anythnig like that here."

"Non, monsieur," added another who had overheard us, "your Constitution has suertainlee nevair been transletted eento any ozzer langveege."

So there we are. That's all of it—and isn't it incredible? The number of foreigners there must be living in the United States who have no English and who, consequently, have never read the Constitution must be staggering.

HERMAN MELVILLE

Moby Dick or, The Whale

From Chapter XLVII, The Mat-Maker

Thus we were weaving and weaving away when I started at a sound so strange, long drawn, and musically wild and unearthly, that the ball of free will dropped from my hand, and I stood gazing up at the clouds whence that voice dropped like a wing. High aloft in the cross-trees was that mad Gay-Header, Tashtego. His body was reaching eagerly forward, his hand stretched out like a wand, and at brief sudden intervals he continued his cries. To be sure the same sound was that very moment perhaps being heard all over the seas, from hundreds of whalemen's lookouts perched as high in the air; but from few of those lungs could that accustomed old cry have derived such a marvellous cadence as from Tashtego the Indian's.

As he stood hovering over you half suspended in air, so wildly and eagerly peering towards the horizon, you would have thought him some prophet or seer beholding the shadows of Fate, and by those wild cries announcing their coming.

"There she blows! there! there! there! she blows! she blows!"

Moby Dick, oder Der weisse Wal

From Vierundzwanzigtes Kapitel

Als wir so in einem for am Weben waren, schreckte ich bei einem seltsamen langgezogenen, wild klingenden und überirdischen Laut auf, so daß mir das Knäuel aus der Hand fiel und ich die Wolken anstarrte, woraus die Stimm emit Flügelschalg zu dröhnen schien. Ganz oben in den Quersalings saß der tolle

Mann aus Gay-Head, Tashtego. Sein Körper streckte sich gierig nach vorn, seine Hand war wie ein Zauberstab ausgebreitet, und in kurzen, plötzlichen Pausen stieß er seine Schreie aus. Gewiß hörte man denselben Laut in demselben Augenblick über die Meere auch anderswo, und Hunderte von Wachtposten, die ebenso hoch in der Luft hingen, stiessen ihn aus. Aber nur von wenigen Stimmen hatte der altbekannte Ruf einen solch merkwürdigen Klang wie vom Indianer Tashtego. Wie er über uns schwebte und Ausschau hielt und wild und raubtiergierig nach dem Horizont starrte, hätte man annehmen können, er wäre ein Prophet oder ein Seher, der die Schatten des Schicksals erblickt hätte und seine Ankunft durch diese wilden Schreie verkünden wollte. "Da bläst sie! Da, dort, da, sie bläst, sie bläst!"

Translated "aus dem Amerikanischen" by Wilhelm Strüver

Moby Dick

From Chapitre XLVII, Le tresseur de nattes

Mêlant en remêlant la trame du tissage, je tressaillis soudain à un son si étrange, si prolongé, si sauvagement et surnaturellement musical, que la pelote du libre arbitre me tomba des mains et que je me mis à regarder les nuages d'où cette voix tombait comme une aile. Haut perché sur les traverses de hune se tenait Tashtego, le fou de Gay-Head. Son corps se penchait en avant impétueusement, sa main se tendait comme une baguette, et, à intervalles brusques et rapides, il reprenait ses cris. Certainement le même son devait à ce moment même être perçu à travers toute l'étendue des mers, poussé par des centaines de pêcheurs de baleines, plantés là-haut, à quetter haut dans les airs à la pointe des mâts; mais il y avait peu de poumons capables de lancer le vieil appel accoutumé avec une cadence aussi marveilleuse que ceux de Tashtego l'Indien.

Tel qu'il se tenait là, planant au-dessus de nous, mi-suspendu

en l'air, épiant tout le tour de l'horizon avec une ardeur si sauvage, on eût pu le prendre pour quelque prophète ou visionnaire
contemplant les ombres du destin et annonçant leur venue par
ses cris sauvages.

"Elle souffle! Là là! là! ... Elle souffle! souffle! souffle!"

Translated by Lucien Jacques, Joan Smith, and Jean Giono

ℭ THIS PASSAGE FROM *Moby Dick* in translation presents two brief
but adequate commentaries on what becomes of whaling in
German and French. They are not meant to be funny, of course—but
aren't they?

I had no idea that I was going to find Tashtego's classic whale-
sighting cry from the masthead translated literally: I had expected
classic French and German cries taking its place.

Until I found it out by looking up "whaling" in several encyclo-
pedias, it had not occurred to me that there was no German or French
whaling—or, at least, there had been none for centuries.

The thing that keeps "Da, dort, da" from sounding quite ridiculous
is that it can at least be howled, where "Là, là, là" can almost only
be barked.

Moby Dick is on a list of books called *Romane der Welt* that were
chosen by Thomas Mann and H. G. Scheffauer to be published in
German. The translation has been cut with discretion and care and
is a very good book. The French version, even though the original
text has not been especially meddled with, gives only the foggiest
effect of Melville and is not very interesting. I do not believe a French
person would disagree with me.

BEATRIX POTTER

PETER RABBIT is "all of a piece." There is no particular excuse for lifting anything in particular from it for quotation. With Peter Rabbit it's all or nothing.

Translations into French, Welsh, and German are all published by Messrs. Frederick Warne & Co., Ltd., of London. They are easily available and will, let us hope, never be out of print.

In French, Peter Rabbit becomes Pierre Lapin, and it is amusing to find Flopsy, Mopsy and Cottontail coming through as Flopsaut, Trotsaut and Queue-de-Coton, and Mr. MacGrégor with an accent.

In German the *vier kleine Hasen* are called, logically enough, Flopsi, Mopsi, Quastchen and Peterchen. Why the German Mr. McGregor is called Herr Krausicke, I don't know.

JAMES STEPHENS

Stephen's Green

The wind stood up and gave a shout.
He whistled on his fingers and

Kicked the withered leaves about
And thumped the branches with his hand

And said he'd kill and kill.
And so he will and so he will.

Les verts de Jacques

Le vent d'un saut lance son cri,
Se siffle sur les doigts et puis

Trépigne les feuilles d'automme,
Craque les branches qu'il assomme.

Je tuerai, crie-t-il, holà!
Et vous verrez s'il le fera!

Translated by James Joyce

Stephen's Green

Der Wind stand auf, liess los einen Schrei,
Pfiff mit den Fingern schrill dabei

Wirbelte duerres Laub durch den Wald
Und haemmerte Aeste mit Riesengewalt.

Zum Tod, heult, zu Tod und Mord!

Und meint es ernst: ein Wind, ein Wort.

Translated by James Joyce

IT WAS NOT UNTIL 1927 that James Stephen and James Joyce happened to discover that they were both born on February 2, 1882. In a belated birthday letter written to Stephens on May 7, 1932, Joyce encloses five translations which he has made of "Stephen's Green." The letter contains some amusing comments about his Latin, German, Italian, and Norwegian translations, but not a word about the French one. Here is part of it:

> Dear Stephens: Here is your poem ["Stephen's Green"] in German, Latin, Norwegian, Italian and French. Can you add your Irish version so as, with the English, to make a rainbow and we might present it to ourselves in a brochure for our jubilee year. . . .
>
> In the German "liess los" sounds rather free and vulgar. It is really "let a shout" but I prefer it to the verb "stossen" which is more elegant. . . .

AFTERWORD

VICTOR PROETZ, 1897–1966

I. A BIOGRAPHICAL NOTE

Born in Saint Louis, Missouri, of German extraction on both sides of his family, Victor Hugo Proetz was the son of William H. Proetz and the brother of the late distinguished otolaryngologist, Dr. Arthur W. Proetz. He received his elementary school education in Saint Louis and later attended the Art Institute of Chicago, where he studied painting and design. Later he enrolled in the architecture course of the Illinois Institute of Technology, where he won a number of awards, including the coveted Emerson Prize. His education was interrupted by World War I, during which he served in the United States Navy. He received his degree in 1923. Later he supplemented his education with two years of travel in France and England.

While Mr. Proetz was primarily a highly gifted architect and interior designer, he was throughout his adult life an accomplished musician and writer. His early professional training was in the office of Samuel A. Marx of Chicago. Later he returned to his birthplace, Saint Louis, where with Ralph Cole Hall he formed the firm of Hall and Proetz. During the years of its existence, from 1924 to 1934, this firm came to have a profound influence on the domestic architecture of the Saint Louis region. In 1930–1931 it received a prize for the public rooms of the Park Plaza Hotel in Saint Louis and as well won acclaim for alterations and additions to the Hotel Adolphus in Dallas, Texas. While in practice in Saint Louis he became a member of the American Institute of Architects.

In 1930 he visited Sweden and there met the great designer Sidney Gibson, the architects Carl Malmsten and Ragnar Östberg, and the sculptor Carl Milles, who many years later was to create for Saint Louis the great fountain called "The Meeting of the Waters." These contacts came at a critical time in Proetz's development and from them he was to continue to derive stimulation for the rest of his life.

In 1934, during a year of study and research in New Haven, he published in *House and Garden* his "Comparative Studies of Regional Architecture in the United States," and in a number of other publications he brought out a variety of articles dealing with contemporary Swedish architecture and decorative arts, the Classic Revival Style in America, and other subjects of a similar nature.

Late in 1934 he joined Mrs. Joshua Cosden of New York as Vice-President of Cosden, Inc. and for almost ten years practiced a combination of architecture and interior design that yielded many of the most distinguished commissions of his career. In London, during 1936–1937, the firm created London's first penthouse, Brook House, for Lord and Lady Louis Mountbatten, later to become the Earl and Countess Mountbatten of Burma. This master work, though not its priceless contents, was unfortunately destroyed during the blitz in World War II.

Throughout the years that followed, Mr. Proetz broadened his repertoire and produced over two thousand designs for furniture, textiles, lighting fixtures, ceramics, and glass; the drawings for many of these, in themselves documents of great distinction and beauty, have been deposited in the Cooper-Hewitt Museum of New York City. Meanwhile, his architectural practice included work in New York City, Long Island, Philadelphia, Lake Forest, Saint Louis, Houston, Palm Beach, and San Francisco. He also executed some interiors for yachts and the officers' quarters for a British aircraft carrier during World War II. His outstandingly successful commissions were probably Brook House in London, a small town house at 7 Sutton Square, New York, for Mrs. Cosden, the furnishings and interiors of a house for his brother, Dr. Arthur W. Proetz, at 12 Westmoreland Place, Saint Louis, and the remodeling of a house in Houston for Mrs.

Oveta Culp Hobby and her husband, Col. William P. Hobby, publisher of the *Houston Post*.

In 1943 Proetz accepted the invitation of Lord and Taylor to become director of the interior decoration department and, under their auspices, opened a large exhibition of architecture and decoration in the spring of 1944. This won wide applause in the daily press as well as in professional publications, and was followed by a one-man show of architecture and decorative arts in the City Art Museum of Saint Louis.

In 1953 he designed and supervised the installation of four interiors of the second half of the nineteenth century as part of the Brooklyn Museum's series of historic American rooms.

In 1961 Mr. Proetz moved to Washington, where he lived until his death in 1966. He held there the title of Curator of Barney Studio House of the Smithsonian Institution and acted as special consultant to the editor of *Museum News*, the official publication of the American Association of Museums. He also designed a series of public rooms and offices for the National Portrait Gallery of the Smithsonian in the old Patent Office building at 8th and F streets in Washington. This was his final work and one which unhappily he did not live to see completed. Thanks to the generosity of his friends and former clients it was possible to furnish the rooms with which Mr. Proetz had been concerned with furniture largely made from his own designs.

On August 20, 1966, he died quietly in Washington. Funeral services were held for him in the National Cathedral.

II. A BRIEF MEMOIR

Though we had once met casually in a purely social fashion, I first really came to know Victor Proetz on the Memorial Day holiday late in May, 1927, when we got together for lunch in downtown Saint Louis. I was at that time a cub architect fresh out of Yale, a draughtsman in one of the distinguished older firms in Saint Louis, and he was a full-fledged partner of Ralph Cole Hall in a firm with a small but notable practice of its own. It was a memorable occasion for me, imbued with the sort of charm and sophistication that made it a veritable eye-opener for a serious-minded youngster like myself. It came just at a time filled with optimism when the world was potentially an oyster only waiting to be shucked by the young and talented. In this age of innocence there was as yet no thought of any economic catastrophe impending, as it was, so near on the horizon.

After a lunch that had been merry and congenial we proceeded to Victor's quarters in an almost deserted office building. There he began to unfold his treasures: all manner of projects that had come to mind in the course of his travels, his school training, and his later practice. Many of these were never to be realized but were far more than merely architectural sketches, and the impact of his vivid imagination, flawless taste, and, above all, complete mastery of the techniques of architectural drawing were to me breathtaking. They were to influence me, no matter what the type of work in which I was engaged, for more than forty years.

Victor was two years older than I and a thousand times more knowledgeable and experienced. Nevertheless he presented his drawings with a mixture of modesty and diffidence that had a unique appeal for one just making his first fumbling start in professional life. The following autumn I joined his office and there experienced the full force of the varied talents with which he had been richly endowed.

Hall and Proetz was a small but by no means undistinguished office. Morale was high and every detail of the commissions entrusted to it received the most meticulous attention. Relations with clients were close and this frequently led to the firm's extending its activities into the realm of furnishing. If this required more time than would have been the case on an ordinary "job," it was by the same token more rewarding and the finished results came nearer the high standards set by the firm. An intimate relationship grew up between the principals and the draughting force that was delightful, and a considerable amount of what was termed "private fun" was indulged in. Granted that it militated against the most efficient carrying out of the firm's commitments and in turn often required overtime on everyone's part, this was taken in stride by one and all without complaint or protest. It was, in fact, a source of great delight to budding draughtsmen, many of whom, as mature designers in their turn, wrote touching letters concerning the memorable times they had so enjoyed as members of the various organizations that Victor headed through the years.

If the daily round was lighthearted, it was never purely frivolous, and there was no doubt that design of the most serious sort was the first order of business, no matter what was under consideration at the moment—a current commission or one of the numerous side issues that added so much to the vivacity of the office routine.

Deeply rooted in the south side of Saint Louis, where a rich and cultivated Teutonic tradition flourished, Victor was fortunate enough to transcend this and to develop formidable creative talents in the fields of music and of literature in addition to his accomplishments in the visual arts. He had, for instance, the gift of being able to produce after a single hearing the subtle popular music appearing in the late twenties and early thirties, and, while he was more than familiar with the great works of the classical composers, took equal pleasure in the lyrics and music of Rodgers and Hart, Vincent Youmans, George and Ira Gershwin, Cole Porter, and Noel Coward. His piano playing afforded infinite delight to his many friends and, one evening, as an experiment, he and a friend composed an architectural verse, complete with architectural jargon and British pronunciations, to the music of Cole Porter's "You're the Top." It went as follows:

> You're the top, you're the drains of Knossos,
> You're the top, you're the Rhodes Colossus,
> You're a marble stair by Philibert de L'Orme,
> You're a Norman choir, you're Chartres' spire,
> You're cruciform!

> You're a dome, you're the nave of St. John,
> You're the home of the honest injun,
> I'm a dernier cri, a Paris Prix, a flop!
> But if, baby, I'm the bottom, you're the top!

In 1928, after a most stimulating tour of duty working on the alterations to the Hotel Adolphus in Dallas, I left Hall and Proetz and

Saint Louis for Boston and remained there for a year and a half, until
the great depression eliminated all but the most securely placed of
the architectural firms. Even these were cut far down in size and I
was one of the many casualties of such shrinkages in staff. It was then
that I learned the hard lesson that architecture is the first profession
to feel an economic flurry and the last to recover from it. I was fortunate enough to be able to translate what ability I had into the field
of teaching and museum work at my alma mater.

But amazingly enough, Hall and Proetz survived and continued to
do brilliant work that brought them awards and recognition in professional publications, and I continued to keep in close touch with
Victor, though often only by letter.

Of course I was only one of a large galaxy of friends and it took
a while for me to realize that he had a way of talking about his many
friends but of keeping them in watertight compartments, so that rela-
tively few of them came to meet one another save through Victor
himself. In spite of his ready wit and gregarious ways at this time, he
was essentially a solitary person and one who relied upon his alone-
ness to give him the quiet he needed to bring into actuality the ideas
that constantly sought an outlet from his fertile and many-sided
mind.

In the course of the years of his greatest fulfillment, he met many
fascinating and interesting people among and through his clients.
His warmest and most faithful friend was undoubtedly Mrs. Joshua
Cosden, with whom he was associated for nine years until the closing
of the firm bearing her name. She understood him completely, was
fond of him personally, and enabled him to realize, while they were
in business together, many projects that would never have gotten off
the drawing board without the connections Mrs. Cosden provided.
The climax of the Cosden years was undoubtedly Brook House in
London, a penthouse created on top of a multi-story apartment
building in Upper Brook Street for Lord and Lady Louis Mountbatten. The commission demanded full time and his presence in London for more than a year, in the course of which he was to meet on
terms of some intimacy many outstandingly interesting men and

women, including several members of the royal family. The great tragedy of his career was of course the destruction of Brook House, his *chef d'oeuvre*, in a London blitz during World War II. For though many outstanding commissions were to come his way after Brook House, none engaged his interest, his peculiar abilities, and his affections to as great a degree as this. Here was an essentially contemporary house furnished with a peerless collection of antique furniture, plus many original designs of his own, and with paintings by famous old masters which Lady Mountbatten had inherited along with the site of Brook House from her grandfather Sir Ernest Cassel.

After the dissolution of Cosden, Inc. in 1943, he went on under the banner of Lord and Taylor to further outstanding accomplishments, but somehow his heart was not wholly engaged and he grew steadily more lonely and isolated in the midst of the busy New York scene. Not that he ever seemed to be downhearted; he was sturdily independent and never idle. But somehow he seemed to lack the aggressiveness that must accompany the "better mousetrap" philosophy.

His modest apartment and office on 52nd Street was still a refuge for friends young and old. Eventually, though, the very fact of his being there, always available, became in itself significant. Days would pass without his leaving his "flat," as he always termed it, save for meals, and these were not always too copious or regular. Though his pride and spirit never flagged, slowly his talents began to be translated into writings of various sorts, many of which were themselves the product of his essential loneliness. His friends began to be concerned and some of them entered into a conspiracy to drop by for frequent visits and even to keep his refrigerator stocked with food.

When out-of-town work had demanded his absence from New York, the sometimes absurd and suggestive names in the local telephone directory caught his eye, and from these he once concocted a complete cast of characters and stage directions for a drawing-room comedy to be set in London and later, while in Houston working on the alterations to the William P. Hobby residence, he composed instructions as to how to build a bathroom, as follows:

Knox. B.   Emily   Peter B. F.E.   Millard J.A.   Kenneth
HOWE to McKAY BASS   ROUEN OTT   OFFEN a TELLER

Betsey R.
VON BOECK

There followed three pages of amusing and explicit rules of what was desirable and necessary in bathroom design and what to be avoided, all concocted in similar fashion from names listed in the telephone directory.

One specific direction goes as follows:

Otto   Calvin   Gilbert Maude   Norma Ray Norma   Joe
LETZ KNOTT have WATT   FRENCH FOLKES   CALL a BIDDY.

Sally T.K.   Alberta Lulu   Harry   William   Laura Mrs. Osa
HIER WEE RILEY DOANE ZIEM to NEEDHAM, DAY ARNDT

Wildon   Novella
NECESSARY   ASHLEY.

Such squibs were photostated and sent around to friends; as a result the "gaiety of nations" level rose a bit. But, almost imperceptibly, he who had contributed intellectually, and materially in a manner he could ill afford, to the growth and development of so many youngsters, himself became a source of some anxiety to many of those who had gone on to win high places in their various fields of endeavor.

In 1961 Victor made a reluctant move to Washington, where he exerted a most beneficial influence on the affairs of the American Association of Museums, then undergoing a transformation that brought it out of a prolonged period of the doldrums. His keen intellect, spirited sense of fun, and high standards of literary performance were just what the Association needed and, though his failing strength was a constant handicap, he made a significant contribution to its affairs. It was in Washington in 1965 that I caught up with him again. Though he was in failing health, he volunteered his services at first and eventually contributed mightily to the transformation of part of the old Patent Office building, masterpiece of the architect Robert Mills and third oldest building in Washington, into the newly established National Portrait Gallery, of which I was at that time director. He died in the summer of 1966 without having

seen his last work completed, but it was here, in the Administrative
Suite, that many of his friends and former clients united to make
these rooms into a memorial to him. They are largely furnished with
pieces of his own design.

To know Victor was a tantalizing experience for the ordinary
person. Though anyone could see that he was delightful and brilliant, he could be and often was the most exasperating of men, and
for no readily perceptible reason. His everyday timetable was the
reverse of that of the usual professional men and women with whom
he had to do business and to whom Victor's hours for creative thinking meant nothing at all. This he passed off lightly, simply remark-
ing that he was a "night-time person." But eventually it took its toll,
for his design was based upon intensive study of the best prototypes
of the sort of project he had in mind at the time. He would seek out
the best source material and spend hours of concentrated study
upon it; and then, when he felt he had absorbed its very essence, the
book would be closed and put away and something that was a dis-
tillation of the period and yet completely fresh would appear on his
drawing board. This was a process that required time, intense con-
centration, and an opportunity to do his work apart from others. The
results were superb, but few people could afford either the time or
the money necessary to achieve them.

There could be no doubt of his capacity, however, or of the
astounding variety of his talents, and his work both in architecture
and the decorative arts was of the highest order and will stand comparison with the best produced by other hands and in other ages.

He was a difficult man to help, and alone he seemed unable to bring
in the large-scale work to which his abilities should have entitled
him. The faultless drawings he created through the years now consti-
tute a monument to his taste and creative ability in the Cooper-
Hewitt Museum of Decorative Arts in New York. His musicianship
and, as a writer, his wit of a great and sometimes merciless subtlety,
all these added strings to his bow. But it was not enough, and one
of the really sad things of his life, for instance, was that for some
twenty years his grand piano lay in a storage warehouse simply because he could not afford to take it out and use it.

When he liked you, Victor was generous to a fault, and many times I have been startled to hear him ascribe to me or to some other of his friends a witty epigram that I knew had come from his own fruitful mind. His friends were legion and ranged from people such as the Mountbattens to the humble but expert cabinetmaker who executed faithfully his extraordinarily meticulous working drawings. All whose paths really crossed his discovered an added zest and delight in life. Even his rivals had respect for his accomplishments, and one rather waspish colleague commented, after examining one of Victor's beautiful working drawings, that "it was so clear that even a journeyman carpenter could have constructed it unaided."

On the whole his life was happy and, while frequently the despair of his friends and well-wishers, he never lost heart and of him it can truly be said that he never did anything he did not want to do or associated with anyone he did not genuinely like. In 1966 he died quietly and courageously, after months of suffering, in Washington, and was buried from the National Cathedral.

It is a happy circumstance that brings at last one of his scholarly and delightful pieces of writing to the attention of the public. That he knew it was to be published pleased him and made him proud. I can only hope that, if his quizzical eye is upon me and is somewhat critical of this brief memorial, the affection and admiration I felt for him will show through and justify my having attempted it.

CHARLES NAGEL

SOURCES

ANONYMOUS: "Rune of Hospitality"

Kenneth Macleod, *The Road to the Isles: Poetry, Lore, and Tradition of the Hebrides* (Edinburgh: Robert Grant & Son, 1927).

Felix Braun, *Die Lyra des Orpheus* (Vienna: Paul Zsolnay Verlag, 1952), p. 591.

Margaret and Deborah Paradise, Ms. (New Haven, 1956).

ANONYMOUS: "The Three Ravens"

Arthur Quiller-Couch, *The Oxford Book of Ballads* (Oxford: At the Clarendon Press, 1910), p. 293.

Wilhelmine Prinzhorn, *Von beiden Ufern des Atlantic* (Halle an der Saale: Verlag von Otto Hendel, 1894), p. 335.

A. Koszul, *Anthologie de la littérature anglais* (Paris: Libraire Ch. Delagrave, 1912).

ANONYMOUS: "Edward, Edward"

Thomas Percy, *Reliques of Ancient English Poetry* (Philadelphia: James E. Moore, 1823; New York: James V. Seaman, 1823), I, 60.

Johann Gottfried von Herder, *Stimmen der Völker in Liedern* (Leipzig: Verlag von Philipp Reklam jun.), p. 144.

Louis Cazamian, *Anthologie de la poésie anglaise* (Paris: Édition Stock, 1946), p. 29.

ANONYMOUS: "Yankee Doodle"

Iona and Peter Opie, *The Oxford Dictionary of Nursery Rhymes* (Oxford: At the Clarendon Press, 1952), p. 439.

Wilhelmine Prinzhorn, *Von beiden Ufern des Atlantic* (Halle an der Saale: Verlag von Otto Hendel, 1894), p. 359.

Nos amis les Alliés; leurs hymnes (Paris: Librairie Hachette et Cie., 1918), p. 6.

W. H. AUDEN: "Look, stranger, on this island now"

W. H. Auden, *The Collected Poetry of W. H. Auden* (New York: Random House, 1945), p. 214.

Georges Albert Astre, *Anthologie de la poésie anglaise contemporaine* (Paris: L'Arche, 1949), p. 127.

Victor Proetz, Ms. (New York, 1956).

JANE AUSTEN: From *Pride and Prejudice*

Jane Austen, *Pride and Prejudice* (London: J. M. Dent & Sons Ltd., 1961; New York: E. P. Dutton & Co., 1961), p. 88.

————, *Les cinq filles de Mrs. Bennett* (Paris: Librairie Plon, 1932), p. 92.

————, *Stolz und Vorurteil* (Zurich: Manesse Verlag, 1948), p. 151.

WILLIAM BLAKE: "The Tiger"

Sir Arthur Quiller-Couch, *The Oxford Book of English Verse* (Oxford: At the Clarendon Press, 1939), p. 577.

Felix Braun, *Die Lyra des Orpheus* (Vienna: Paul Zsolnay Verlag, 1952), p. 610.

Félix Rose, *Les grands lyriques anglais* (Paris: H. Didier, Éditeur, 1940), p. 99.

M. L. and Philippe Soupault, *William Blake, Chants d'innocence et d'expérience* (n. p.: Édition Charlot, 1947), p. 69.

RUPERT BROOKE: "The Soldier"

Rupert Brooke, *The Collected Poems of Rupert Brooke* (New York: John Lane Company, 1916), p. 111.

Felix Braun, *Die Lyra des Orpheus* (Vienna: Paul Zsolnay Verlag, 1952), p. 728.

Henri-Marcel et Michel Bernfeld, *Poètes anglo-américaine des deux guerres* (Paris: Presses Universitaires de France, 1947), p. 29.

ELIZABETH BARRETT BROWNING: From *Sonnets from the Portuguese*

Elizabeth Barrett Browning, *Sonnets from the Portuguese* (Mount Vernon: Peter Pauper Press, n.d.).

Rainer Maria Rilke, *Übertragungen, Gesammelte Werke* (Leipzig: Insel-Verlag, 1930), VI, 7, 12, 28.

André Maurois, *Sonnets from the Portuguese, avec une traduction en vers français et une introduction,* (New York: Brentano's, 1944), pp. 42, 52, 83.

ROBERT BROWNING: Song from *Pippa Passes*

Sir Arthur Quiller-Couch, *The Oxford Book of English Verse*, (Oxford: At the Clarendon Press, 1939), p. 869.

Robert Browning, "Pippa passe," *La Revue Hebdomadaire* (June, 1900), p. 241.

Felix Braun, *Die Lyra des Orpheus* (Vienna: Paul Zsolnay Verlag, 1952), p. 669.

ROBERT BURNS: "Auld Lang Syne"

Robert Burns, *The Complete Poetical Works of Robert Burns*, (Boston and New York: Houghton Mifflin Company, 1897), p. 251.

Félix Rose, *Les grands lyriques anglais* (Paris: H. Didier, Éditeur, 1940), p. 81.

William Jacks, *Robert Burns in Other Tongues* (Glasgow: James Mac-Lehose and Sons, 1896), p. 89.

LORD BYRON: "She walks in beauty"

I. Braham and I. Nathan, *A Selection of Hebrew Melodies Ancient and Modern* (London: I. Nathan, 1815), p. 3.

Herman Behr, *Perlen englisher Dichtung in deutcher Fassung* (Dresden: E. Pierson's Verlag), p. 51.

Félix Rose, *Les grands lyriques anglais* (Paris: H. Didier, Éditeur, 1940), p. 135.

LEWIS CARROLL: From *Alice's Adventures in Wonderland*

Lewis Carroll, *Alice's Adventures in Wonderland* (London: Macmillan and Co., 1866).

————, *Alice's Abenteuer im Wunderland*, translated by Antonie Zimmermann (London: Macmillan and Co., 1869).

————, *Aventures d'Alice au pays des merveilles*, translated by Henri Bué (London: Macmillan and Co., 1869).

LEWIS CARROLL: "Jabberwocky"

Lewis Carroll, *Through the Looking-Glass, and What Alice Found There* (Mount Vernon: Peter Pauper Press, n.d.).

Dr. Robert Scott ("Thomas Chatterton"), "Der Jammerwock," *Macmillan's Magazine*, XXV (February, 1872).

Frank Lord Warrin, Jr., "Le Jaseroque," *The New Yorker*, January 10, 1931, p. 52.

GEOFFREY CHAUCER: From *Canterbury Tales*

Geoffrey Chaucer, *Canterbury Tales,* edited by John Matthews Manly (New York: Henry Holt and Company, 1928), p. 149.

———, *Geoffrey Chaucers Canterbury-Erzählungen, nach Wilhelm Hertzbergs Übersetzung neu herausgegeben von John Koch* (Berlin: Herbert Stubenrauch/Verlagsbuchhandlung, 1925), p. 3.

———, *Les contes de Canterbury* (Paris: Félix Alcan, 1908).

SAMUEL TAYLOR COLERIDGE: "Kubla Khan"

Samuel Taylor Coleridge, *The Poems of Samuel Taylor Coleridge* (London: Humphrey Milford, Oxford University Press, 1940), p. 297.

Felix Braun, *Die Lyra des Orpheus* (Vienna: Paul Zsolnay Verlag, 1952), p. 629.

Louis Cazamian, *Anthologie de la Poésie anglaise* (Paris: Édition Stock, 1946), p. 204.

E. E. CUMMINGS: "the hours rise up"

E. E. Cummings, *Collected Poems* (New York: Harcourt, Brace and Company, 1938).

Eugéne Jolas, *Anthologie de la nouvelle poésie américaine* (Paris: Kra, 6 rue Blanche, 1928), p. 50.

Victor Proetz, Ms. (New York, 1956).

CHARLES DICKENS: From *A Christmas Carol*

Charles Dickens, *The Works of Charles Dickens* (New York: Charles Scribner's Sons, 1905).

———, *Les apparitions de Noël* (Paris: Librairie d'Amyot, 1847).

———, *Wehnachtsgeschichten* (Berlin: Hermann Seemann Nachfolger, Verlagsgesellschaft, n.d.).

EMILY DICKINSON: "I lost a world the other day"

Emily Dickinson, *The Poems of Emily Dickinson* (Boston: Little, Brown and Company, 1937), p. 173.

Fernand Baldensperger, *D'Edmond Spenser à Alan Seeger,* Vol. XIII of *Harvard Studies in Comparative Literature* (Cambridge, Mass.: Harvard University Press, 1938), p. 83.

Victor Proetz, Ms. (1955).

T. S. ELIOT: "Sweeney among the Nightingales"

T. S. Eliot, *Collected Poems, 1909–1935* (New York: Harcourt, Brace and Company, 1936), p. 65.

———, *Poèmes 1910–1930*, translated by Pierre Leyris (Paris: Éditions du Seuil, 1947), p. 79.

W. S. GILBERT: From *The Mikado*

W. S. Gilbert and Arthur Sullivan, *The Mikado, or The Town of Titipu* (London: Chappell & Co., 1885).

———, *Der Mikado, oder Die Stadt Titipu* (Chicago: Louis W. H. Neebe, 1887).

THOMAS JEFFERSON: From the Constitution of the United States

James M. Beck, *La constitution des États-Unis* (Paris: Librairie Armand Colin, 1923), p. 206.

L. P. Conseil, *Mélanges politiques et philosophiques extraits des Mémoires et de la correspondance de Thomas Jefferson* (Paris: Paulin, Libraire-Éditeur, 1833), I, 127.

François Rodolphe Dareste de la Chavanne, *Les constitutions modernes: Europe, Afrique, Asie, Océanie, Amérique; traductions accompagnées de notices historiques et de notes explicatives par F. R. Dareste et P. Dareste* (Paris: Librairie du Receuil Sirey, 1928–1934), VI, 34–66.

Notes documentaires et études (Paris: Presidence du Conseil, Secrétariat Général du Gouvernement, Direction de la Documentation, 1945– , no. 253 [March 7, 1946]).

Le Marquis de Talleyrand-Périgord, *Étude sur la Republique des États-Unis d'Amerique* (New York: Hurd & Houghton, 1876).

Franz Friese, *Amerikanische Verfassung und Regierung* (Frankfort: H. Reinhardt, 1947).

Karl Loewenstein, *Vom Wesen der amerikanischen Verfassung* (Frankfort: W. Metzner, 1950).

Dr. G. A. Zimmermann, *Vierhundert Jahre amerikanischer Geschichten* (Milwaukee: Verlag von Geo. Blumder, 1893), Appendix.

HERMAN MELVILLE: From *Moby Dick*

Herman Melville, *Moby Dick or, The Whale* (New York: The Modern Library, 1950), p. 214.

———, *Moby Dick, oder Der weiße Wal* (Berlin: Verlag von Th. Knaur Nachf., 1929 [?]), p. 98.

———, *Moby Dick* (Paris: Librairie Gallimard, 1941), p. 220.

JAMES STEPHENS: "Stephen's Green"

James Joyce, *Letters of James Joyce*, edited by Stuart Gilbert (New York: The Viking Press, 1957).